PREPARING FOR THE
MARK
OF THE
BEAST

Preparing for the Mark of the Beast

Copyright ©2006 by Midnight Call Ministries
Published by The Olive Press a subsidiary of Midnight Call Inc.
Columbia, South Carolina, 29228

Copy Typist: Lynn Jeffcoat
Copy Editor: Susanna Cancassi
Proofreaders: Angie Peters, Susanna Cancassi
Layout/Design: Michelle Kim
Lithography: Simon Froese
Cover Design: Michelle Kim

Library of Congress Cataloging-in-Publication Data

Froese, Arno
Preparing for the Mark of the Beast
ISBN #978-0-937422-63-2

1. Prophecy   2. Bible Teaching

Printed in the United States of America

CONTENTS

INTRODUCTION

Programming the Mark of the Beast

In order to fully grasp God's overall message to mankind, we must think long-term. We mustn't allow ourselves to become influenced by circumstances or events taking place today or in recent history. For that reason we will not go into detail about the latest technological inventions that could hasten the fulfillment of the prophecy about the Mark of the Beast. Speculations are dangerous and misleading, because the Mark of the Beast will be implemented only after the Church of Jesus Christ, the light of the world and the salt of the earth, has been removed.

We will, therefore emphasize preparation of the Mark, which will climax in the final stages of the fulfillment of Revelation 13:15: "And he had power to give life unto the image of the beast, that the image of the beast should both speak, and cause that as many as would not worship the image of the beast should be killed."

We will begin our analysis with Abraham, which means we must travel back in time approximately 4,000 years. God used Abraham to initiate His plan of salvation. With Abraham, God prepared a way for man to escape eternal damnation. This brings up an important question: Couldn't God have just used Abraham to accomplish that goal by allowing Sarah to conceive a child supernaturally in order to bring forth the Son of God and implement God's plan of salvation from the very start? Why did it take more than 2,000 years for the Savior to be born? Why hasn't the Church, which is almost 2,000 years old, been raptured yet? Why didn't God establish the 1,000-year kingdom of peace right away? Why is the preparation taking so long? These and many other questions fail to acknowledge that God is compassionate and merciful. His time is not our time and the Bible says that His ways are beyond understanding. Therefore, we will not find satisfactory answers to these types of questions while we are here on earth. But what we can do is search the Scripture to see for ourselves how God deals with mankind and how He, step by step, implements His plan of salvation and His intention to fully restore His creation to its original order. Exodus 34:6 describes God as being merciful and gracious, longsuffering, and abundant in goodness and truth.

God is not a dictator. He has graciously given people the free will either to obey Him and live, or to disobey Him and die. No one in all of human history ever will be able to justify his disobedience to Almighty God.

Furthermore, we often fail to realize that God is timeless. The Apostle Peter wrote: "one day is with the Lord as a thousand years, and a thousand years as one day" (2 Peter 3:8). That fact throws all of our mathematical configurations right out the window! Nothing makes sense anymore when you understand that God can stretch one day into 1,000 years and can compact those thousand years into one day. That contradicts our way of thinking. God, in His infinite wisdom, had a plan long before Abraham. Ephesians 1:4 testifies: "he hath chosen us in him before the foundation of the world."

On the other side of the story is Satan, the father of lies, who is God's enemy. He must be destroyed, not by brute force but by the truth: "whom the Lord shall consume with the spirit of his mouth and shall destroy with the brightness of his coming" (2 Thessalonians 2:8). In order for that to happen, world history had to be brought into existence.

On one hand we see God preparing a way for man to escape from eternal damnation and on the other hand we see Satan's desire for the human race to end in eternal damnation.

The Bible prophesies that the majority of mankind will refuse to believe in God; subsequently, those unbelievers will end up eternally damned. The minority will accept God's invitation to receive forgiveness of their sins, based on Jesus' shed blood. Those who believe will be born again; they become new creatures in Christ.

God revealed His plan of salvation to the serpent, who had deceived Adam and Eve: "I will put enmity between thee and the woman, and between thy seed and her seed; it shall bruise thy head, and thou shalt bruise his heel" (Genesis 3:15). With the words "I will," "it shall," and "thou shalt," preparation became a reality.

Abraham is a key person God used in preparation for salvation. He is referred to in the New Testament as the father of all believers.

Here is how God dealt with Abraham: "And he said unto Abram, Know of a surety that thy seed shall be a stranger in a land that is not theirs, and shall serve them; and they shall afflict them four hundred years" (Genesis 15:13). Again we see that time is not an issue with God. Instead of the promised Savior coming right away, Abraham's descendants were promised to be enslaved in a foreign nation for 400 years. Yet in the same breath God said: "Unto thy seed have I given this land, from the river of Egypt unto the great river, the river Euphrates" (Genesis 15:18). In other words, the future is already a "done deal" with God!

That prophecy was made in 2047 B.C., yet the Exodus took place in April of 1446 B.C.. Israel entered the Promised Land 40 years later, in 1407 B.C. Thus, 640 years are sandwiched between the promise made to Abram, "unto thy seed have I given this land," and the Israelites' actual entry into the land.

One more point that teaches us how to understand the preparation for the Mark is found in Daniel 2, where we read about a great image that symbolizes the entire history of the Gentile nations:

> Thou, O king, sawest, and behold a great image. This great image, whose brightness was excellent, stood before thee; and the form thereof was terrible. This image's head was of fine gold, his breast and his arms of silver, his belly and his thighs of brass, His legs of iron, his feet part of iron and part of clay. Thou sawest till that a stone was cut out without hands, which smote the image upon his feet that were of iron and clay, and brake them to pieces. Then was the iron, the clay, the brass, the silver, and the gold, broken to pieces together, and became like the chaff of the summer threshingfloors; and the wind carried them away, that no place was found for them: and the stone that smote the image became a great mountain, and filled the whole earth (Daniel 2:31-35).

This speaks about a period of approximately 3,000 years; yet, the events described in this passage are seen as one compact event. In fact, verse 44 says: "And in the days of these kings shall the God of heaven set up a kingdom, which shall never be destroyed." Here are three millennia compacted into "days." This fact further reinforces God's timelessness in view of earth's limited time.

It takes 3,000 years to prepare for the kingdom of God to be accomplished on earth. But what is written will be fulfilled: "Thy kingdom come. Thy will be done in earth as it is in heaven" (Matthew 6:9).

Meanwhile, God's enemy must establish his counterfeit kingdom. According to Bible prophecy, Satan will be successful. Revelation 13:8 reveals: "all that dwell upon the earth shall worship him."

The important difference between the eternal God and the devil is revealed in one word: time. Revelation 12:12 says: "Therefore rejoice, ye heavens, and ye that dwell in them. Woe to the inhabiters of the earth and of the sea! for the devil is come down unto you, having great wrath, because he knoweth that he hath but a short time."

Please keep God's timelessness and Satan's limited time in mind when you read this book. Satan is using the time he has left to program the Mark of the Beast. That will be the pinnacle of his achievements.

Chapter 1

PREPARING ABRAHAM

In order for God to fulfill His promises to bring forth the Savior, He contacts Abram: "Now the LORD had said unto Abram, Get thee out of thy country, and from thy kindred, and from thy father's house, unto a land that I will shew thee: And I will make of thee a great nation, and I will bless thee, and make thy name great; and thou shalt be a blessing: And I will bless them that bless thee, and curse him that curseth thee: and in thee shall all families of the earth be blessed" (Genesis 12:1-3).

Abram is the beginning of Israel and he is also the beginning of faith; thus, he is referred to in the New Testament as the father of all believers. Note that through the avenue of faith, Abram became the father of the nation of Israel. Israel is the point of physical contact between heaven and earth. Israel is God's ambassador to the world. This fact should help us better understand Jesus' words: Salvation is of the Jews.

To reinforce the statement that Israel is the contact

between heaven and earth, we must read Zechariah 8:3: "Thus saith the LORD; I am returned unto Zion, and will dwell in the midst of Jerusalem: and Jerusalem shall be called a city of truth; and the mountain of the LORD of hosts the holy mountain."

To implement God's intention to "dwell in the midst of Jerusalem," He had to make a beginning, and that beginning was with Abram, the preparation for the establishment of a visible, physical kingdom on planet Earth. Why did God select Abram? Because he unconditionally believed in God.

Enemy Kingdom

It stands to reason, therefore, that the enemy of God likewise must prepare to solidify his kingdom by persuading mankind to worship him instead of God. He will accomplish that by implementing the Mark of the Beast. Jesus said, "My kingdom is not of this world: if my kingdom were of this world, then would my servants fight, that I should not be delivered to the Jews: but now is my kingdom not from hence" (John 18:36). Satan is the king of this earthly kingdom. He has authority over all sinners. The Bible says all have sinned, which means all belong to the kingdom of the devil. Subsequently, Satan could offer this world to Jesus: "Then was Jesus led up of the spirit into the wilderness to be tempted of the devil... Again, the devil taketh him up into an exceeding high mountain, and sheweth him all the kingdoms of the world, and the glory of them; And saith unto him, All these things will

I give thee, if thou wilt fall down and worship me"
(Matthew 4:1,8,9).

Abram's Calling

As we read earlier, Abram's calling is recorded in
Genesis 12:1-3, where God said He would do four
things. He would:
1. Show Abram a country
2. Make Abram a great nation
3. Bless Abram, who in turn, would be a blessing to
the whole world
4. Bless those who blessed Abram and curse those
who cursed him

Abram: The Silent Prophet

We read nothing in Scripture about Abram's own
will, intention or plan. Not one word is recorded of
Abram verbally responding to God's calling. He asked
no questions, expressed no disagreements and stated
no doubts. The next verse begins with Abram's action:
"So Abram departed, as the LORD had spoken unto
him" (verse 4).

What is significant is that Abram did not experience
any supernatural miracles. No signs and wonders
accompanied his walk with God. That's the kind of
faith we must possess today: believing without seeing.

Arrival in Canaan

Abram was 75 years old when he left Haran, the
place where he had gone with his father. He had stayed

in Haran until his father had died. Then he, Sarai and Lot finally went to Canaan.

Again, we read nothing about Abram speaking a word. Why didn't he have anything to say? Because he believed in the One who is the author and finisher of all things, the One who spoke the world and all of creation into existence. Abram recognized that there was no need to do anything but to obey God's instructions.

The Altar and the Promise

"And the LORD appeared unto Abram, and said, Unto thy seed will I give this land: and there builded he an altar unto the LORD, who appeared unto him" (Genesis 12:7). Again, no words of Abram are recorded, nor are any instructions given. We read only promises.

We read of the second altar in verse 8: "And he removed from thence unto a mountain on the east of Bethel, and pitched his tent, having Bethel on the west, and Hai on the east: and there he builded an altar unto the LORD, and called upon the name of the LORD." One can immediately sense that this man's primary target was focused upon the God of heaven. Hebrews 11:10 testifies: "For he looked for a city which hath foundations, whose builder and maker is God." Although no words are recorded, we do read that Abram "called upon the name of the LORD" (verse 8). But the content of his prayer was hidden; it was between him and his God.

An Unsure Step

Abram had been instructed to go to Canaan, and he obeyed. He received the deed to the Promised Land. But then: "Abram journeyed, going on still toward the south. And there was a famine in the land: and Abram went down into Egypt to sojourn there; for the famine was grievous in the land" (verses 9-10). What is missing? Abram did not ask God for direction, nor did he receive any instruction from God about making his next move. He headed south to Egypt apparently based upon his own initiative.

Abram's First Recorded Words Were A Lie

"And it came to pass, when he was come near to enter into Egypt, that he said unto Sarai his wife, Behold now, I know that thou art a fair woman to look upon: Therefore it shall come to pass, when the Egyptians shall see thee, that they shall say, This is his wife: and they will kill me, but they will save thee alive. Say, I pray thee, thou art my sister: that it may be well with me for thy sake; and my soul shall live because of thee" (verses 11-13). Abram's first recorded words were a lie. He asked his wife to participate in his conspiracy: "Say, I pray thee, thou art my sister."

It may be argued that Sarai was actually Abram's half-sister, but that doesn't justify his actions, because he revealed the motive of his conspiracy. Apparently the Egyptian would have killed Abram had he known Sarai was his wife.

But God did not desert Abram; instead, He intervened on his behalf. Thus, we read in verse 17: "And the LORD plagued Pharaoh and his house with great plagues because of Sarai Abram's wife." As a result, "Pharaoh commanded his men concerning him: and they sent him away, and his wife, and all that he had" (verse 20).

Abram Returns

Abram returned to where he had begun: "Unto the place of the altar, which he had made there at the first: and there Abram called on the name of the LORD" (Genesis 13:4).

What a mighty prophecy for our times! When we go our own way and it leads to disappointment, and even tragedy, complaining about our predicament will not help. The only solution is to return to the altar where we first met the Lord. He is our comfort, the answer to all of our problems and failures. Do you remember the day you asked the Lord to save you? Do you remember the joy that flooded your heart and soul? That is the meeting place to which you must return.

Lot's Separation

In his initial calling, Abram was instructed to leave his country, relatives and his father's house, but when he departed for the journey, he had a companion. Lot went with him. We do not know why, but the fellowship between the one who was called and the one who tagged along developed into an open conflict. "And

Lot also, which went with Abram, had flocks, and herds, and tents. And the land was not able to bear them, that they might dwell together: for their substance was great, so that they could not dwell together. And there was a strife between the herdmen of Abram's cattle and the herdmen of Lot's cattle: and the Canaanite and the Perizzite dwelled then in the land" (Genesis 13:5-7).

Actually there was no need for Lot's herdsmen to argue with Abram's. Lot should have intervened and told his men to give Uncle Abram first priority. After all, he was the one who had received a direct calling from God, and he was the one who obeyed that calling. But that did not happen; the opposite took place: "And Abram said unto Lot, Let there be no strife, I pray thee, between me and thee, and between my herdmen and thy herdmen; for we be brethren. Is not the whole land before thee? separate thyself, I pray thee, from me: if thou wilt take the left hand, then I will go to the right; or if thou depart to the right hand, then I will go to the left" (verses 8-9). Here we see Abram's generosity exemplified. He wasn't selfish. God personally had given the entire land to Abram, yet Abram gave his nephew Lot the first choice of land.

Why was Abram so generous? Because he believed in God's promise to give the land to him and his descendants. That was sufficient. The present unpleasant circumstances were insignificant to Abram.

Lot, on the other hand, acted upon what he could see: "And Lot lifted up his eyes, and beheld all the plain of Jordan, that it was well watered every where, before the LORD destroyed Sodom and Gomorrah, even as the garden of the LORD, like the land of Egypt, as thou comest unto Zoar. Then Lot chose him all the plain of Jordan; and Lot journeyed east: and they separated themselves the one from the other" (verses 10-11).

After Lot chose his territory, we read a shocking statement in verse 13: "But the men of Sodom were wicked and sinners before the LORD exceedingly."

Here we are reminded to walk by faith and not by sight. Second Corinthians 4:18 explains: "While we look not at the things which are seen, but at the things which are not seen: for the things which are seen are temporal; but the things which are not seen are eternal."

The First Holy Land Tour

Now Abram received a reconfirmation: "And the LORD said unto Abram, after that Lot was separated from him, Lift up now thine eyes, and look from the place where thou art northward, and southward, and eastward, and westward: For all the land which thou seest, to thee will I give it, and to thy seed for ever. And I will make thy seed as the dust of the earth: so that if a man can number the dust of the earth, then shall thy seed also be numbered. Arise, walk through the land in the length of it and in the breadth of it; for I will give it unto thee" (Genesis 13:14-17). Abram had to take possession of the land by faith, although he was an old man whose wife was well beyond child-bearing years. Here again we see the Lord's "I will:"

- "I will give it unto thee."
- "I will make thy seed as the dust of the earth."
- "I will give it unto thee."

Once again, no recorded dialogue took place between God and Abram. The Lord reconfirmed His promises to Abram very personally and Abram remained silent.

Lot's Trouble

War broke out after Lot had separated from Abram. "And the vale of Siddim was full of slimepits; and the kings of Sodom and Gomorrah fled, and fell there; and they that remained fled to the mountain. And they took all the goods of Sodom and Gomorrah, and all their victuals, and went their way. And they took Lot, Abram's brother's son, who dwelt in Sodom, and his goods, and departed" (Genesis 14:10-12). War resulted in a blessing for the victor and a curse for the loser. The winner took all.

Abram to the Rescue

In Lot's case, the enemies defeated Sodom but did not take possession of the land. Instead, they took all of the valuables, the livestock and the people, and led them captive to their place of origin.

Abram was informed: "And when Abram heard that his brother was taken captive, he armed his trained servants, born in his own house, three hundred

23

and eighteen, and pursued them unto Dan. And he divided himself against them, he and his servants, by night, and smote them, and pursued them unto Hobah, which is on the left hand of Damascus" (Genesis 14:14-15). What an incredible rescue operation! Keep in mind the distance between Sodom and Dan was more than 250 kilometers or 150 miles. This was an extremely difficult undertaking. With his small army of only 318 soldiers, Abram was able to defeat the army that had defeated Sodom.

More amazing is that he rescued every soul and all of the property: "And he brought back all the goods, and also brought again his brother Lot, and his goods, and the women also, and the people" (verse 16).

Abram, Sodom and Melchizedek

Abram returned to Sodom, where he was met by the king: "And the king of Sodom went out to meet him after his return from the slaughter of Chedorlaomer, and of the kings that were with him, at the valley of Shaveh, which is the king's dale" (verse 17).

Apparently, Abram ignored the king of Sodom because in the next verse, we read: "And Melchizedek king of Salem brought forth bread and wine: and he was the priest of the most high God. And he blessed him, and said, Blessed be Abram of the most high God, possessor of heaven and earth: And blessed be the most high God, which hath delivered thine enemies into thy hand. And he gave him tithes of all" (verses 18-20).

Melchizedek, the mysterious king of Salem, presented to Abram the substance of salvation: bread
and wine. Later in history, Jesus broke the bread,
gave it to His disciples and said: "Take, eat; this is my
body" (Matthew 26:26). Then He took a cup, gave it
to them, and said: "Drink ye all of it; For this is my
blood of the new testament, which is shed for many
for the remission of sins" (Matthew 26:27-28).

Abram received a prophetic demonstration of the
coming victory of Jesus.

A Work of Grace

We must keep in mind that Abram saved people
who did not deserve to be saved. We already read that
"the men of Sodom were wicked and sinners before
the LORD exceedingly" (Genesis 13:13). Here we
are reminded that Christ died for us while we were
yet sinners: He loved us first.

We must never become so arrogant that we begin
to think we were worth saving, that some shred of
good in us made us worthy of the sacrifice that pur-
chased our salvation. That is the gospel of the
Antichrist, a teaching that unfortunately is being
preached the world over, even among some fundamental Christian Bible-believers.

These teachers attempt to instill pride and an
inflated sense of self-worth into the minds of their
congregants. Their message is logical: "You are worth
being saved: in fact, you are so worthy that God paid
the ultimate price for your redemption!" But that is

so far from what we read in the Word of God. Our salvation is based completely on His grace. He loved us first, but not because we were worthy of being loved. This little difference harbors major implications. When we try to add just one iota of self-worth to our salvation, then we are actually detracting from the perfect work of Christ on Calvary's cross.

Melchizedek, the Priestly King

Who was King Melchizedek of Salem? We know that Salem means Jerusalem and Melchizedek means "King of righteousness." This mysterious king was also a priest. We read of the "order of Melchizedek" in Psalm 4, which means "likeness in official dignity." We know that the law prohibited a king from exercising the office of priest. Saul, Israel's first king, took this office upon himself and was rejected by God as Israel's king.

Hebrews 7:3 identifies King Melchizedek with the following words: "Without father, without mother, without descent, having neither beginning of days, nor end of life; but made like unto the Son of God; abideth a priest continually." According to this passage of Scripture, some scholars have said that King Melchizedek was a pre-incarnate appearance of the Lord Jesus Christ. But the Bible does not confirm this because we read that this man was "made like unto the Son of God." There is a likeness, but that is as far as we can take this line of thinking.

The King of Sodom

"And the king of Sodom said unto Abram, Give me the persons, and take the goods to thyself" (Genesis 14:21). Now the king of Sodom enters the picture again. Something strange occurred in this meeting between Abram and the king: We see no evidence that the king of Sodom showed thankfulness for his freedom, but instead he propositioned Abram: "give me the persons and take the goods to thyself." Thus, the king typifies man's self-centeredness. That didn't go over too well with Abram: "Abram said to the king of Sodom, I have lift up mine hand unto the LORD, the most high God, the possessor of heaven and earth, That I will not take from a thread even to a shoe-latchet, and that I will not take any thing that is thine, lest thou shouldest say, I have made Abram rich" (verses 22-23).

Abram sensed the evil spirit of Sodom. He would not want to have taken favors from the king in any manner, shape or form. Under no circumstances would he want to align himself with the king of Sodom and his people. The rescue of the people from Sodom and the return of all their goods was only a "coattail" blessing that resulted from Abram's rescue of Lot.

Gentiles Included

Abram's action illustrates prophetically the inclusion of the Gentiles in God's plan of salvation. Jesus came for His people, the Jews, and offered them eternal salvation. The Apostle Paul repeatedly emphasized in his letters that the Gospel was to go to the Jews first. To those from among the Gentiles, he wrote: "That at that time ye were without Christ, being aliens from the commonwealth of Israel, and strangers from the covenants of promise, having no hope, and without God in the world" (Ephesians 2:12). Nothing can possibly be worse than being without hope and without God. However, the next verse begins: "But now in Christ Jesus ye who sometimes were far off are made nigh by the blood of Christ" (verse 13).

Abram's Concern About the Future

After many years, Abram starts to realize that God's promise had not yet been fulfilled: "And Abram said, Lord GOD, what wilt thou give me, seeing I go childless, and the steward of my house is this Eliezer of Damascus? And Abram said, Behold, to me thou hast given no seed: and, lo, one born in my house is mine heir" (Genesis 15:2-3). These are the words of a man who trusted God for numerous years. He waited patiently to present his concern to God. How did the Lord answer? "And he brought him forth abroad, and said, Look now toward heaven, and tell the stars, if thou be able to number them: and he said unto him, So shall thy seed be" (verse 5). That was good enough for Abram. Verse 6 states: "And he believed in the LORD; and he counted it to him for righteousness."

Faith in the living Word of God was one of Abram's trademarks. His was not a faith built upon experiences, prayers or miracles; it was simply faith in the God who spoke to him.

Abram Becomes Abraham

Abram's name change is significant because it high-lights the contrast between Satan and God. God is the creator; therefore, He gave Abram a new name. Satan is not the creator; therefore, he cannot give people a new name. He can only give his followers a number. The devil will give his people the Mark of the Beast.

Here is how Abram's name change took place: "And when Abram was ninety years old and nine, the LORD appeared to Abram, and said unto him, I am the Almighty God; walk before me, and be thou per-fect. And I will make my covenant between me and thee, and will multiply thee exceedingly. And Abram fell on his face: and God talked with him, saying, As for me, behold, my covenant is with thee, and thou shalt be a father of many nations. Neither shall thy name any more be called Abram, but thy name shall be Abraham; for a father of many nations have I made thee" (Genesis 17:1-5). Abram means "high father" or "father of height," obviously signifying his contact with the God of heaven. Abraham means "father of a multitude." That certainly must have seemed strange because this man was 99 years old and had no chil-dren! Yet God's promises are sure; they will come to pass in His own timing.

Abram's name had to be changed because he was destined to fulfill God's promise that he would become "a father of many nations." This was a physical impossibility but a spiritual reality. With this name change, God prophetically demonstrated that the old person — the flesh and blood — cannot inherit the kingdom of God. Something new must be created to receive the inheritance; thus, the new name.

We must add here that not only Abram, but also Sarai would undergo a name change: "And God said unto Abraham, As for Sarai thy wife, thou shalt not call her name Sarai, but Sarah shall her name be" (Genesis 17:15). God intended to do something new. Sarah would bear a son, Isaac, who would father a son, Jacob. (He, too, had his name changed when Jacob, "deceiver," became Israel "warrior of God.")

By now, we should realize that preparation, even thousands of years before the fulfillment, is of utmost importance. Yes, God could have done everything instantaneously, but He chose to create history, thousands of years, in order to provide salvation for mankind just as He had said: "I will put enmity between thee and the woman, and between thy seed and her seed; it shall bruise thy head, and thou shalt bruise his heel" (Genesis 3:15).

Chapter 2

PREPARING ISRAEL

J ust as Abraham had to go through a period of preparation, his descendants, which God named "Israel," had to go through a process of preparation as well. As a matter of fact, at this very moment, Israel is being prepared in numerous ways, but particularly to meet the One they crucified. That will be the moment of their collective salvation. Before becoming a nation, Israel had to serve as slaves in Egypt for 400 years. But that was not enough. Then they had to wander, seemingly aimlessly, in the wilderness for another 40 years. They experienced God's judgment several times during their pilgrimage to the land that flowed with milk and honey, the Promised Land. That was all part of the process they underwent in order to become a nation that would ultimately fulfill God's intention.

At this time, God has not fulfilled all His promises to Israel. The original promise to Abraham — "And

I will make of thee a great nation, and I will bless thee, and make thy name great; and thou shalt be a blessing: And I will bless them that bless thee, and curse him that curseth thee: and in thee shall all families of the earth be blessed" (Genesis 12:2-3) — has only been fulfilled spiritually. This is documented in Galatians 3:7-8: "Know ye therefore that they which are of faith, the same are the children of Abraham. And the scripture, foreseeing that God would justify the heathen through faith, preached before the gospel unto Abraham, saying, In thee shall all nations be blessed."

When we read the details, for example in Deuteronomy 15:6, we know that has not been fulfilled yet: "For the LORD thy God blesseth thee, as he promised thee: and thou shalt lend unto many nations, but thou shalt not borrow; and thou shalt reign over many nations, but they shall not reign over thee." But as surely as the first part has been fulfilled, manifested in the creation of His Church, so the last part also will be fulfilled in due time.

The present condition of Israel doesn't change God's eternal resolutions. For example, "For thou art an holy people unto the LORD thy God: the LORD thy God hath chosen thee to be a special people unto himself, above all people that are upon the face of the earth" (Deuteronomy 7:6). The Jews are a holy people, regardless of their present condition-which, to be quite honest, is rather deplorable, particularly from a moral perspective. God has chosen them nevertheless as His special people; that cannot be changed by anyone in this world or even by the devil himself.

Not only are the Israelites special, but they are "above all people that are upon the face of the earth." Will that prophecy be fulfilled? Absolutely. Israel has gone through a preparation process that will continue until God has fulfilled His purpose with His people.

Israel's Enemies

Now we should better understand why the world rejects Israel, some openly, others secretly. But one cannot deny that Israel stands alone when it comes to the promises regarding the Promised Land. No nation on earth officially agrees to recognize the borders for Israel as set forth in the Bible. And no nation sanctions Israel's sovereignty over its capital city, Jerusalem.

From the very day of Israel's establishment to the present day, calls for Israel's violent destruction have been emphatic and continuous across the Middle East. Some examples:

2006: Iranian president declared: "Israel must be wiped off the map." Many international leaders reacted appropriately with shock and horror but that's all they did. Yet tragically, such statements in the Arab/Islamic world are nothing new.

2005: Egyptian Muslim Brotherhood leader Muhammad Mehdi Akef, "I declared that we will not recognize Israel which is an alien entity in the region. And we expect the demise of this cancer soon."

2005: PA Sheikh Ibrahim Mudeiris: "The Jews are a virus resembling AIDS. The day will come when everything will be relieved of the Jews. Listen to the Prophet Muhammad, who tells you about the evil end that awaits Jews. The stones and trees will want the Muslims to finish off every Jew."

2001: Former Iranian President Hashemi Rafsannani, "If a day comes when the world of Islam is duly equipped with the arms Israel has in possession, the strategy of colonialism would face a stalemate because application of an atomic bomb would not leave anything in Israel."

1993: PLO Chairman Yasser Arafat: "Since we cannot defeat Israel in war we do this in stages. We take any and every territory that we can of Palestine, and establish sovereignty there and we use it as a springboard to take more. When the time comes, we can get the Arab nations to join us for the final blow against Israel." [same day of Oslo signing ceremony]

1980: PLO Chairman Yasser Arafat: "Peace for us means the destruction of Israel. We are preparing for an all-out war, a war which will last for generations."

1967: Iraqi President Abdar-Rahman Aref: "The existence of Israel is a mistake that must be rectified. The clear aim is to wipe Israel off the map."

1959: Egyptian President Gamal Abdul Nasser: "I announce from here, on behalf of the United Arab Republic people, that this time we will exterminate Israel."

1954: Saudi King Saud: "The Arab nations should sacrifice up to 10 million of their 50 million people, if necessary, to wipe out Israel. Israel is to the Arab world a cancer to the human body."

1948: Arab League Secretary-General Azzam Pasha: "This will be a war of extermination and a momentous massacre which will be spoken of like the Mongolian massacres and the Crusades."

Examples like these are rampant. As the record shows, loathing of Jews and Israel and a desire to destroy them have not evaporated because of formal peace treaties with Egypt and Jordan, the Oslo peace process, the creation of the Palestinian Authority (PA) or land handed over by Israel or anything else. Quite the opposite is true: Arab and Muslim rejection of Israel has spread across the globe so that even in the gentlemanly halls of American academe, professors like the late Edward Said of Columbia University and Tony Judt of New York University have openly embraced the idea of dismantling Israel. (*Zionist Organization of America*, by Morton A. Klein and Dr. Daniel Mandel.)

It is not surprising that the devil is so keenly interested in infiltrating all nations in order to make each nation think it is special. Consider what the devil was able to do under the leadership of Adolf Hitler in Germany by calling the Germans to be the "master race." Satan wanted to supplant the Jews. That's just what Hitler attempted to do: annihilate the Jewish race. Satan stands behind the nations of the world.

Preparing for the Birth of the Messiah

"But thou, Bethlehem Ephratah, though thou be little among the thousands of Judah, yet out of thee shall he come forth unto me that is to be ruler in Israel; whose goings forth have been from of old, from everlasting" (Micah 5:2).

Another key part of the process of preparation is the coming of our Lord Jesus Christ Himself. The prophets spoke about His coming, and wrote down certain signs that would occur before His coming. Daniel prophesied the exact time of His death in chapter 9, Isaiah declared He would be born of a virgin, and Micah identified Bethlehem as the geographic location of the Messiah's birth.

Another prophecy was made approximately 1,450 years before the birth of Christ: "The LORD thy God will raise up unto thee a Prophet from the midst of thee, of thy brethren, like unto me; unto him ye shall hearken" (Deuteronomy 18:15).

Micah identified Bethlehem as the exact geographic location of the Messiah's birth: "Therefore the Lord himself shall give you a sign; Behold, a virgin shall conceive, and bear a son, and shall call his name

Immanuel" (Isaiah 7:14). This prophecy was made in 740 B.C.

Preparations had to be made even in the final moments before the birth of Christ. Joseph and Mary lived in Nazareth, but Jesus had to be born in Bethlehem, according to Bible prophecy. The family had to move to Bethlehem in order to fulfill this prophecy. Every person who lived in the Roman Empire had to return to his or her place of birth to be registered. That means the entire Roman world was moved so that Jesus could be born in Bethlehem!

In 700 B.C. the prophet Isaiah provided this detail about the Messiah, who would be despised and rejected, and who would die: "For he was cut off out of the land of the living: for the transgression of my people was he stricken" (Isaiah 53:8).

When we study this closely, we become amazed by the details, including the location of His burial: "he made his grave with the wicked, and with the rich in his death" (Isaiah 53:9). Jesus died between two criminals and was buried in a rich man's cave.

Fulfilled!

An immense volume of documentation is available relating to the fulfillment of Bible prophecy. For instance, Matthew 1:22-23 reads: "Now all this was done, that it might be fulfilled which was spoken of the Lord by the prophet, saying, Behold, a virgin shall be with child, and shall bring forth a son, and they shall call his name Emmanuel, which being interpreted is, God with us."

Not long after the Child was born, the family had to flee to Egypt: "And was there until the death of Herod: that it might be fulfilled which was spoken of the Lord by the prophet, saying, Out of Egypt have I called my son" (Matthew 2:15).

The prophet Jeremiah wrote about the slaughter of the innocent baby boys in Bethlehem: "Then Herod, when he saw that he was mocked of the wise men, was exceeding wroth, and sent forth, and slew all the children that were in Bethlehem, and in all the coasts thereof, from two years old and under, according to the time which he had diligently inquired of the wise men. Then was fulfilled that which was spoken by Jeremy the prophet" (Matthew 2:16-17).

Jesus grew up in Nazareth: "And he came and dwelt in a city called Nazareth: that it might be fulfilled which was spoken by the prophets, He shall be called a Nazarene" (verse 23). These few verses clearly show that prophecy recorded in the Old Testament is fulfilled in the New Testament. This is all a part of God's plan of salvation and that plan requires time to be fulfilled.

Tax Time

The pregnant virgin lived in Nazareth, not Bethlehem. During those days, Caesar Augustus ordered the taxation or registration of all Roman citizens:

> And it came to pass in those days, that there
> went out a decree from Caesar Augustus, that all
> the world should be taxed. (And this taxing was

first made when Cyrenius was governor of Syria.) And all went to be taxed, every one into his own city. And Joseph also went up from Galilee, out of the city of Nazareth, into Judea, unto the city of David, which is called Bethlehem; because (he was of the house and lineage of David:) To be taxed with Mary his espoused wife, being great with child. And so it was, that, while they were there, the days were accomplished that she should be delivered. And she brought forth her firstborn son, and wrapped him in swaddling clothes, and laid him in a manger; because there was no room for them in the inn (Luke 2:1-7).

Believing the Prophetic Word

The New Testament confirms that the religious authorities in Jerusalem believed in the fulfillment of Bible prophecy. They quoted Scripture when they asked the Wise Men from the East, "Where is he that is born King of the Jews?"... "And they said unto him, In Bethlehem of Judea: for thus it is written by the prophet, And thou Bethlehem, in the land of Judah, art not the least among the princes of Judah: for out of thee shall come a Governor, that shall rule my people Israel" (Matthew 2:2,5-6).

They indeed believed in the Scripture, but not in the immediacy of the fulfillment. If so, they would have gone to Bethlehem to seek and worship the Child. But the religious people who were in charge of the temple and the implementation of the law had forged a cozy relationship with Rome's political authority. They thought the king wasn't on the scene yet, because, they believed, a king could only be authorized by the Roman government. They already had one, King Herod. If Jesus was the King, then there would be a conflict.

Nation at Stake

We see the conflict manifest during Jesus' ministry. We read the following testimony in John 11:47-48: "Then gathered the chief priests and the Pharisees a council, and said, What do we? for this man doeth many miracles. If we let him thus alone, all men will believe on him: and the Romans shall come and take away both our place and nation." The chief priest and Pharisees were afraid to lose their jobs. Thus we see that you can believe Scripture, but if you don't believe in the immediacy of its fulfillment, then you may be missing the point. The rejection of Jesus as the Messiah of Israel was part of the preparation process.

The Apostle Paul later explained: "Have they Israel stumbled that they should fall? God forbid: but rather through their fall salvation is come unto the Gentiles, for to provoke them to jealousy" (Romans 11:11). In verse 28 he wrote: "As concerning the gospel, they are enemies for your sakes: but as touching the election, they are beloved for the fathers' sakes." God's plan of salvation for Israel had to be placed on hold temporarily for one reason: so the Gentiles could be saved.

James explained this in Acts 15:13-17:

> And after they had held their peace, James answered, saying, Men and brethren, hearken unto me: Simeon hath declared how God at the first did visit the Gentiles, to take out of them a people for his name. And to this agree the words of the prophets; as it is written, After this I will return, and will build again the tabernacle of David, which is fallen down; and I will build again the ruins thereof, and I will set it up: That the residue of men might seek after the Lord, and all the Gentiles, upon whom my name is called, saith the Lord, who doeth all these things.

In view of these and many more facts we will discuss later, we do well to cautiously analyze Scripture apart from a human time frame. In other words, the Church from among the Gentiles will be completed in due time, which will cause the Church to be raptured from planet Earth, the devil and his angels be cast to the earth, the Great Tribulation will begin and, in the end, Israel will be saved.

Chapter 3

PREPARING THE WORLD

In Chapter 1 we saw the preparation process that took place with Abraham, the father of believers. We also noticed the promises God made to him. In Chapter 2 we discussed the preparation of Israel, particularly in relation to the birth of the Messiah.

From Scripture we know that the Mark of the Beast will be implemented in due time. To get our bearings on the subject, let us read: "And he causeth all, both small and great, rich and poor, free and bond, to receive a mark in their right hand, or in their foreheads: And that no man might buy or sell, save he that had the mark, or the name of the beast, or the number of his name" (Revelation 13:16-17).

All the people who live on the earth will be registered and properly categorized. This is essential for a global society to function; therefore, we do not deal with the issue of "if" the Mark will be implemented, only of "when." All who have eyes to see and ears to hear realize that we are approaching that time at warp speed.

Recent History

I like to use the example of our ministry's first purchase of an electronic calculator in 1970 to show the amazing technological progress being made today. That calculator cost about $135 and weighed just over 4 pounds. This machine could do nothing more than the four basic functions: addition, subtraction, division and multiplication. The salesman traveled more than 35 miles from Cincinnati to our office in Hamilton, Ohio to demonstrate this electronic "miracle." Needless to say, we were quite proud to become owners of such a modern piece of office equipment.

Now compare that to today's electronics. Any discount store sells $20 watches that tell the time, date, day, month, year, and that can be used as alarm clocks, stop watches, appointment reminders, and calculators. That's quite a jump from our 4-pound $135 limited function-adding machine!

This illustrates that we live at a time when the development of electronic-based technology is virtually exploding. Modern electronics easily make it possible to identify all people and mark them with the coming and dreadful Mark of the Beast.

The Genesis of Computers

Although neither the implanted chip nor the computer is the direct manifestation of the Mark of the Beast, I fully believe that these and many other electronic gadgets are part of the process in preparing for the Mark of the Beast.

A computer search of electronic inventions revealed 1935 as the year the computer was invented by a man named Konrad Zuse (1910-1995), a construction engineer for the Henschel Aircraft Company in Berlin, Germany at the beginning of World War II. Zuse earned the semiofficial title of "inventor of the modern computer" for his series of automatic calculators, which he invented to help him with his lengthy engineering calculations. Zuse has modestly dismissed the title while praising many of the inventions of his contemporaries and successors as being equally if not more important than his own (http://inventors.about.com/library/weekly/aa050298 .htm.)

Next in line came the ABC Computer, dated 1942:

Professor John Atanasoff and graduate student Clifford Berry built the world's first electronic-digital computer at Iowa State University between 1939 and 1942. The Atanasoff-Berry Computer represented several innovations in computing, including a binary system of arithmetic, parallel processing, regenerative memory, and a separation of memory and computing functions.It seemed significant that these early inventors were not at all eager to claim the title as the inventors. Atanasoff said: "I have always taken the position that there is enough credit for everyone in the invention and development of the electronic computer"

(http://inventors.aqbout.com/library/blcoindex.htm.).

The invention and progress of the computer

touched off a virtually unending process of inventions.

The November 2003 edition of *National Geographic* headlined an article entitled "Watching You: The World of High-Tech Surveillance," which summarizes:

> The future is here where cameras can film you wherever you go, where your cell phone can signal exactly where you are, where one glance can reveal exactly who you are. Sometime soon — in an airport, in the lobby of your office, in your bank — a scanner might get a glimpse of your eyes and a computer reveal your identity. For iris-recognition technology you can thank the owner of this face, computer scientist John Daugman (he's wearing specially made contact lenses imprinted with digital maps of his own irises). His creation is just one of the technologies revolutionizing public surveillance. (By David Shenk, November 2003, *National Geographic*).

These and many other interesting articles are only the tip of the computer-based technology iceberg. Although the computer's origin can be traced back to 1935, it was virtually unseen to the general public until approximately 40 years later. Now, with literally hundreds of millions of technicians and computer scientists working on inventions, who knows what already has been accomplished today that won't be publicized until 10 or 20 years from now?

I believe the Mark of the Beast will be such an amazing and miraculous invention that even the skeptics will fall for the deception. In other words, people will quickly realize the tremendous benefits of the system of identification for the good of themselves and their respective societies.

Toward Total Control

We all have experienced the benefits of computers, whether at home, in school or business. The world has literally opened up so that anyone in the world can connect to any other place on earth. All the knowledge in the libraries of the world is now at our fingertips. But computers using bar codes and scanners to keep accurate control of products is only the beginning stages of the ultimate use of the computer. Eventually, the computer will be used to seize total control over humanity.

Take, for example, the problems of illegal immigrants, drug traffickers, terrorists and criminals. Wouldn't anyone want to live in a crime-free society where all pay their share of taxes, no one steals from others and crooked deals are eliminated? But how can that be achieved? The answer looks almost too simple: electronic control.

In the same way we now control import and export, identify products by the hundreds of millions, if not trillions, such applications can be used to register every person on earth. That would be the first step towards eliminating the many crimes we hear reported daily through our news media.

47

Proper registration and identification of everyone will cause total control to be implemented. To understand this simple process, one only needs to look at the so-called third-world countries. What is their biggest problem? Identity! Usually the governments in those countries have very little information about the citizens, thus crime abounds, black-market economy thrives, and national corruption hinders progress. As a result, investors shy away from such countries and foreign currency does not flow in their direction. The world's wealthiest and most successful nations are those that have as much information as possible about their citizens. Thus they quickly know how citizens react to certain laws and how to implement changes quickly.

Today, for the first time in history — because of computer technology — every government in the world can thoroughly identify each person. (Hence the fear of many people about the government's ability to gather too much personal information.) But gathering all the identification information requires time, and that is what preparation is all about: teaching the masses that proper identification and information will finally improve their quality of life so that they will become willing to follow even the dictates of unreasonable requirements. Therefore, the Mark of the Beast will be a crowning achievement of man's intelligence. The success will cause the fulfillment of Revelation 13:16-17: "And he causeth all, both small and great, rich and poor, free and bond, to receive a mark in their right hand, or in their foreheads: And that no man might buy or sell, save he that had the mark, or the name of the beast, or the number of his name."

The Imitator of God

God is the creator of all things. Satan tries to duplicate His work. If we ask where Satan got the idea for the Mark of the Beast, we must search the Bible. There we will find the answer, "Satan himself is transformed into an angel of light" (2 Corinthians 11:14). Satan is the father of lies, the murderer from the beginning: "He was a murderer from the beginning, and abode not in the truth, because there is no truth in him. When he speaketh a lie, he speaketh of his own: for he is a liar, and the father of it" (John 8:44).

Satan has to come up with an identification system that will mimic God's. This should not surprise us because his intention is clearly revealed in Isaiah 14:13-14: "For thou hast said in thine heart, I will ascend into heaven, I will exalt my throne above the stars of God: I will sit also upon the mount of the congregation, in the sides of the north: I will ascend above the heights of the clouds; I will be like the most High."

When the Word of God became flesh and Jesus Christ lived on earth, we read of Satan revealing his intention again: "Again, the devil taketh him up into an exceeding high mountain, and sheweth him all the kingdoms of the world, and the glory of them; And saith unto him, All these things will I give thee, if thou wilt fall down and worship me. Then saith Jesus unto him, Get thee hence, Satan: for it is written, Thou shalt worship the Lord thy God, and him only shalt thou serve" (Matthew 4:8-10).

There should be no doubt in anybody's mind about the identity of the god of this world. It is Satan, the father of lies. He is the master deceiver who has made all people on planet Earth buy into his philosophy: "I will be like the most High."

Often we hear people say that Satan will be deceiving the whole world, but the truth is that Satan has already deceived the world. The world is already following him. Those who haven't accepted Christ as Savior are part of Satan's kingdom. They reject the teaching of the Bible that every person is a sinner in need of a Redeemer; therefore, Satan's attacks are directed against those who faithfully hold to the promise and truths of Holy Scripture.

In summary, Satan inspires people to produce their own salvation and thereby build his own kingdom of peace. But in the process of doing so, he must present his plan to be the most fitting to the mind and desires of sinful man. The Antichrist, therefore, will be Satan's masterpiece; he will be a man according to the heart of man.

Preparing Man's Heart

The Mark of the Beast will not occur overnight. But preparation is well under way. Another key part of that preparation involves making human hearts ready to accept the coming endtime system. One way that is being accomplished is through the media and entertainment industries, which are shaping moral and ethical codes of behavior — through fiction mixed with facts — 365 days a year in the privacy of each person's home. (And we must add, most people love it!)

Fictional characters have become particularly important in the process of eroding society's sense of morality. These characters have gotten such a grip on such a large portion of the population that many people no longer seem to be able to distinguish the real from the fake! Further, movies, television, and music teach people to believe that they can do the impossible — and that they can do it apart from the control of God.

The Church in Transgression

Needless to say the United States is the world's undisputed leader of the entertainment and information industry. Therefore, it should not be too surprising that the United States holds the title in several other rather unpleasant championships: crime, drugs, pornography and violence. Even worse, the US leads the industrialized world in divorce, the greatest destroyer of the family. And worse yet, divorce among evangelical Christians occurs more frequently than it does among the rest of the population.

The greatest catastrophe, however, is that the

Church at large, particularly evangelical Christians, is hypocritical about this fact. Instead of repenting, many Christians are in the forefront fighting for "biblical morals." They are trying to force so-called biblically based laws upon the public at large, yet they themselves are breaking them. In other words, the transgressors are trying to tell sinful and lost people to follow in their footsteps. What blasphemy to the precious name of our Lord Jesus Christ! No wonder so many voices can be heard calling Christians hypocrites. Unfortunately, this is often a fair assessment.

Instead of preaching the Word of God, living a life that is pleasing to the Lord and bringing our flesh in daily subjection to the Spirit, evangelical leaders have become the modern-day Pharisees. That, my friend, is one of the greatest tragedies in the United States of America.

Media Power

This brings us to an important question: Does the entertainment industry actually possess power over U.S. citizens? Is it fair to place at least partial responsibility upon the entertainment industry for the destruction of the family? Can we in good conscience say that the entertainment industry is the sponsor of pornography, immorality, drugs and crime? Who is to blame for the U.S. being the headquarters for crime, with the highest prison population in the world?

These are difficult questions to answer and cannot be dealt with in an arbitrary manner. However, it is important to investigate this issue because if the entertainment and communication industries are at least partially responsible for this "Hall of Evil Fame," then it stands to reason that this same system can be successfully implemented to deceive any nation into believing virtually anything.

Admittedly, it is difficult to prove that the entertainment industry is responsible for the moral decline of a nation, but we cannot deny that it subjects viewers to immoral teaching.

The Invisible Battle

In relation to this fact, let us see what the Bible has to say about our battle: "For we wrestle not against flesh and blood, but against principalities, against powers, against the rulers of the darkness of this world, against spiritual wickedness in high places" (Ephesians 6:12). We are fighting an invisible enemy, the prince of darkness, who entices us to live in the flesh, thus resulting in the fulfillment of Galatians 5:19-21: "Now the works of the flesh are manifest, which are these; adultery, fornication, uncleanness, lasciviousness, idolatry, witchcraft, hatred, variance, emulations, wrath, strife, seditions, heresies, envyings, murders, drunkenness, revellings, and such like: of the which I tell you before, as I have also told you in time past, that they which do such things shall not inherit the kingdom of God."

Therefore, if what we see and hear does influence us to the extent that we begin to believe in them, then it stands to reason that the media has the power to present a religion led by a false Jesus, empowered by a false spirit, proclaiming a false gospel.

One thing is sure: the world will eventually be deceived by the power of the Antichrist and his false prophet so that Revelation 13:8 will be fulfilled: "all that dwell upon the earth shall worship him" [Antichrist].

Mass Communication

The words, "and all the world wondered after the beast," reveal a unique prophecy: All will have to become one and all will praise and admire this new global leader, now made visible and audible through television, internet, and movies to all people everywhere.

Until a certain point in history, no one could speak to his or her own county or city, let alone the entire world. Addressing audiences larger than a few thousand people was impossible. Mass communication became possible for a larger group of people with the invention of the printing press in the 1400s. But even then it was very expensive and not many people were able to read. For instance, a printed Bible could cost as much as a year's wages. As time went on, however, newspapers began to be published and exhibited in town squares where larger numbers of people could read and be informed. But the real breakthrough in communication came when Italian electronic engineer Guglielmo Marconi discovered radio waves in

1895. For the first time in history, a message could be sent over the air and received by anyone with a receiver.

Communication became even more personal with the invention of the television, based on German physicist Paul Nipkow's theory, in 1884. Now audio and visual communications could travel directly to each individual home. That became the most significant step toward programming any and all segments of the population.

What does all that have to do with the Mark of the Beast? A lot. This is all part of the preparation that leads to the universal education of all people — with its positive as well as negative ramifications.

I am aware of the value of television and the accuracy in which we receive news reports about our nation and other parts of the world; however, the possibility that it could be used to brainwash the masses cannot be denied and must not be ignored.

Television and Politicians

How can a political candidate win an election? What source of communication must he or she use in order to earn the confidence — and the votes — of potential voters? I think we all know the answer. The candidate must convince television viewers that they will benefit if the candidate is elected.

That means the candidate needs to present ideas in a way that will make the majority agree with him. Thus, the candidate cannot be totally truthful; he or she cannot be honest, and must be able to dodge any questions that may be controversial. A candidate who is unable to do so will lose voters. This type of political promotion was impossible only a short time ago, but it is essential today.

Television Rules

We all agree that television is a tool that is successfully employed for both good and bad. But we cannot deny the amazing power television has over people — even over those who only watch news broadcasts and nature shows. Any successful global business that sells a product without utilizing television is virtually non-existent.

Think about the fast food industry. Television brings "food" right into your living room. The viewer has little power to resist the cleverly manipulated offer, and as a result, that product becomes desirable. Important to add here is that food promotion, for example, is not based on reality. Advertisements and commercials feature photos that have been artistically styled to appear fantastically delicious. This can be said for many other products as well. They are presented to us in a totally unrealistic way, yet we fall for the deception; we buy the products.

TV Addiction

Do you have power over your television? Could you turn it off for a year? Six months? How about one month? From the information gleaned by various surveys, most people who have decided to turn off the television end up caving in after two or three days.

A century ago, people had time to do things with their families, read books, play games with their children, go on picnics, and attend social functions. Many of those activities have been replaced by the television sets in the middle of our living rooms.

TV is a major contributing factor towards our total dependency on electronics. It is part of the preparation for the Mark of the Beast.

Partial Truth

Television has become the dictator of the family, the god in our homes. Unfortunately this becomes embarrassingly clear during social visits. Instead of talking with one another, people tend to turn on the TV. Virtually all programs have been designed for one purpose: to get viewers "hooked" on a particular program.

Even a simple weather forecast can be exciting. Well before a scheduled weather forecast, announcements "tease" viewers into staying tuned to the broadcast. And to make the weather forecast even more dramatic, forecasters have added elements such as "heat index" and "wind chill factor" to measuring temperature.

Global Political Correctness

News from any part of the world is transmitted directly into our living rooms; thus, we are informed about the things that are happening in the world. But is that really true? It's only partly true as we cannot always trust the sources to be accurate and unbiased.

For example, ask the average U.S. citizen if he or she would like to live in Europe, and most will answer, "No, they have so many problems and I would be too afraid to live there." How can they make such a statement? Because they were educated by a "politically correct" news media. They have allowed the news media to become the unquestioned authority. However, if they took a little time to do some research, they would quickly find that it is significantly more dangerous to live in the United States than in Europe.

What about Israel? For decades, when the news media has reported a terrorist activity in Israel, a large percentage of those planning to come on one of our Israel tours have called immediately to cancel their reservations. Yet by comparison, it is 19 times more dangerous to live in Detroit than in Jerusalem.

But facts and statistics become irrelevant as brainwashing begins to take hold. That is a part of the progressive preparation for the Mark of the Beast.

Chapter 4

SPIRITUAL REALITIES

Before we continue our discussion relating to the coming Mark of the Beast, it is important to realize that we are dealing with spiritual realities. Here is what we read in 2 Corinthians 4:18: "While we look not at the things which are seen, but at the things which are not seen: for the things which are seen are temporal; but the things which are not seen are eternal." Keep these words in mind: "things which are not seen are eternal." We are confronted with visible realities 24 hours a day — not only at home and at work, but even while we sleep. We dream about things we have experienced, read about or seen. But spiritual things are what this chapter and this book are all about.

The preparation for the Mark of the Beast is a spiritual undertaking of the forces of evil. In due time, it will become a visible reality here on earth.

Thus it is with the Church of Jesus Christ. We are a minority consisting of born-again persons the world over. Each one of us belongs to a different family, we live all over the world, and we have different nationalities, culture, languages, color of skin, and traditions. But we constitute the Body of Christ. We are totally one in the Lord Jesus Christ, who is the head of the Body.

Nothing can be seen of this Church as far as visible manifestations are concerned because they are *in* the world but not *of* the world. Thus we too are involved in a progress of preparation not for this earth, but for heaven.

"Thy Brother Shall Rise Again"

In John 11 we find the story about Lazarus, the brother of Mary and Martha, who lived in the town of Bethany. Jesus received a message that Lazarus was sick. Something strange is then reported in verse 6: "When he heard therefore that he was sick, he abode two days still in the same place where he was." Jesus deliberately did not go to visit His sick friend. Then we read in verse 11: "These things said he: and after that he saith unto them, Our friend Lazarus sleepeth; but I go, that I may awake him out of sleep." With these words, Jesus totally ignored a physical reality by pointing to a spiritual one. The disciples still did not understand. They said, "Lord, if he sleep, he shall do well" (verse 12). But then verse 14 states: "Then said Jesus unto them plainly, Lazarus is dead."

Finally, Jesus went to Bethany and was met by Lazarus' sister, Martha, who heard this message:

"Thy brother shall rise again" (verse 23). Martha obviously was familiar with Scripture and knew about the resurrection: "I know that he shall rise again in the resurrection at the last day" (verse 24). Then follows Jesus' statement regarding spiritual reality: "I am the resurrection, and the life: he that believeth in me, though he were dead, yet shall he live: And whosoever liveth and believeth in me shall never die. Believest thou this?" (verses 25-26).

Of course Lazarus did die again, but that was only physical death. Spiritually, the promise is solid: "whosoever...believeth in me...shall never die." Jesus totally ignores earthly, physical and visible realities by emphasizing the spiritual reality, which clearly reveals immortality of the soul.

"They That Be With Us Are More"

Let's look at another example from the Old Testament book of 2 Kings 6. Elisha was in the city of Dothan and the king of Syria with his armed forces. We read in verse 14: "Therefore sent he thither horses, and chariots, and a great host: and they came by night, and compassed the city about." That was a visible reality; this is testified by Elisha's servant: "And when the servant of the man of God was risen early, and gone forth, behold, an host compassed the city both with horses and chariots. And his servant said unto him, Alas, my master! how shall we do?" (verse 15). How did Elisha answer? "Fear not, for they that be with us are more than they that be with them" (verse 16). Next a tremendous spiritual reality is revealed: "And Elisha prayed, and said, LORD, I pray thee, open his eyes, that he may see. And the LORD opened the eyes of the young man; and he saw: and, behold, the mountain was full of horses and chariots of fire round about Elisha" (verse 17). Suddenly, visible realities were overshadowed by spiritual realities. Thus we must learn to realize that all things we receive with our five senses are temporary, but the invisible is what counts. That is what the Bible is all about.

Understanding Prophecy

Prophecy begins with faith. But what is faith? Hebrews 11:1 defines faith as "the substance of things hoped for, the evidence of things not seen." That powerful statement is rather strange because invisible evidence is not recognized in a court of law. Therefore, when we speak of prophecy, we must view it from a different perspective, and that is through the perspective of faith: "the evidence of things not seen."

We have the evidence in Scripture that people will receive the Mark of the Beast, that there will be an image of the beast manufactured by people, but at this point, we don't see it. This, too, is evidence of things not seen.

The Church, as we will see a little later, is the Body of Jesus Christ. It is also defined as the temple of the Holy Spirit, yet no one can identify the Church of Jesus Christ on earth. We can point to church buildings or denominations and say they are the Church.

But that, as we all know, is not according to Scripture. Therefore, the true Church consisting of only born-again believers is still evidence not seen yet.

We, too, find ourselves in the time of preparation and that preparation is for the moment when we will see Him as He is. We will change from believing to seeing.

Let's set the stage for being able to differentiate between the heavenly and the earthly and better understand "the evidence of things not seen."

A simple example may help. Take any object of weight, hold it in your hand, and release it. It will fall to the ground. This demonstration shows that anything that has weight will fall to the ground if released. This is a scientific fact, based on gravity: What goes up must come down. But this scientific fact does not apply in space, where there is no up and down. Therefore, we can safely say that there is a science applicable to earth and a science applicable to space. We must never mix these two; otherwise, confusion will result. The Bible is a heavenly book but it speaks primarily about the earth, particularly about the earth's future.

Another example: All elevations are measured from the level of the ocean because water remains perfectly level. Or does it? Let's fly an airplane 40,000 feet above the earth, and what do we see? We notice that the earth below us is curved. Thus, water definitely does not remain perfectly horizontal. Therefore, our scientific fact has changed because we are looking at it from a different location.

Let's take another step further and view planet Earth from a spaceship. Viewed from several hundred kilometers above the earth, we see only a round globe. Actually, from that perspective, the words "above" and "below" cease to exist. An absolute scientific fact on earth becomes an absolute non-scientific fact in space.

The Heavenly Book

We already said the Bible is a heavenly book authored by God with a message addressed to mankind. In order to understand this message we must become heavenly, which means we must learn to understand what God is saying from a heavenly perspective.

Only through the Holy Spirit can we receive what God intends us to understand. The Apostle Peter wrote: "For the prophecy came not in old time by the will of man: but holy men of God spake as they were moved by the Holy Ghost" (2 Peter 1:21).

These holy men did not write the passages of Scripture by themselves; they were moved by the Holy Spirit. Jesus promised the disciples that when the Comforter came, He would bring back all the memories: "But the Comforter, which is the Holy Ghost, whom the Father will send in my name, he shall teach you all things, and bring all things to your remembrance, whatsoever I have said unto you" (John 14:26).

Thus, these holy men who wrote the Scripture were men of faith, they believed what they received and therefore they presented it to us in the pages of the Bible as "evidence of things not seen."

If you are not a believer in Jesus Christ, then you can read the words in the Bible and you may understand the historic reports, names, places, objects, actions and dates, but you will never understand the real message God intends to convey to you.

The Apostle Paul described people without faith: "But the natural man receiveth not the things of the Spirit of God: for they are foolishness unto him: neither can he know them, because they are spiritually discerned" (1 Corinthians 2:14).

The New Person

How do we obtain this faith? Jesus said: "whosoever believeth in him should not perish, but have eternal life" (John 3:15). Believing in Jesus is the key to becoming a spiritual person — that is, born again. Nicodemus, who came to Jesus at night wanting to have his questions answered, heard these words: "Verily, verily, I say unto thee, Except a man be born again, he cannot see the kingdom of God" (John 3:3). Note the word "see." That speaks about a person's spiritual eyes. When you become born again of the Spirit of God, you begin to see the kingdom of God and everything else falls in place. You may not understand a particular prophecy about how things will shape up, but with your rebirth, you are on the right track toward your eternal home.

Jesus made the distinction between the visible and the invisible world crystal clear in verse 6: "That which is born of the flesh is flesh; and that which is born of the Spirit is spirit."

Have You Been Born Again?

Have you been born again of the Spirit of God? I'm not asking whether you have made a decision for Christ or uttered the sinner's prayer. I'm specifically asking whether you have been born again. Doubtless, there is much confusion regarding that question. I fear for the countless souls who have made an emotional decision but who, in reality, have never broken through to a living faith in Jesus to become born again of His Spirit. This is quite evident from the various popular teachings that do not correspond to Holy Scripture. In fact, these teachings contradict the Bible in various ways. You are responsible for the decision you make, and this is the most important decision in your life because it means either eternal salvation or eternal damnation.

Sign of the Rebirth

Midnight Call Ministries offers a booklet by Dr. Wim Malgo entitled, *Seven Signs of a Born-Again Person*. Here is an abbreviated excerpt:

> **Sign 1:** The born-again person knows he or she is a child of God: "The Spirit itself beareth witness with our spirit, that we are the children of God" (Romans 8:16).

Sign 2: The life of a born-again person becomes visible. Jesus said in Matthew 7:16, "Ye shall know them by their fruits," and not by church membership.

Sign 3: The born-again person has a spirit of prayer and is no longer "dead through trespasses of sins" (Ephesians 2:1). Instead, Romans 8:26 becomes a reality: "Likewise the Spirit also helpeth our infirmities: for we know not what we should pray for as we ought: but the Spirit itself maketh intercession for us with groanings which cannot be uttered."

Sign 4: The born-again person hungers for the Word of God. Jesus said, "I am the bread of life" (John 6:48). A born-again person will seek the Scripture, "Search the scriptures; for in them ye think ye have eternal life: and they are they which testify of me. And ye will not come to me, that ye might have life" (John 5:39-40).

Sign 5: The born-again person will suffer adversity. We read in John 16:33: "These things I have spoken unto you, that in me ye might have peace. In the world ye shall have tribulation: but be of good cheer; I have overcome the world." A born-again person learns to rejoice in tribulation.

Sign 6: The born-again person experiences victory over temptation and sin. Romans 8:1 reads: "There is therefore now no condemnation to them which are in Christ Jesus, who walk not after the flesh, but after the Spirit." A spiritual walk is required for achieving constant victory. Paul wrote: "But thanks be to God, which giveth us the victory through our Lord Jesus Christ" (1 Corinthians 15:57).

Sign 7: The born-again person waits with joy and expectancy for the return of Jesus Christ. To the disciples, Jesus said: "And when these things begin to come to pass, then look up, and lift up your heads; for your redemption draweth nigh" (Luke 21:28). First Corinthians 1:7 says: "So that ye come behind in no gift; waiting for the coming of our Lord Jesus Christ." And Hebrews 9:27 states: "And as it is appointed unto men once to die, but after this the judgment."

There is one more item I would like to add: the reality of the spiritual life. Let us read 2 Corinthians 4:8-10: "We are troubled on every side, yet not distressed; we are perplexed, but not in despair; persecuted, but not forsaken; cast down, but not destroyed; always bearing about in the body the dying of the Lord Jesus, that the life also of Jesus might be made manifest in our body." Note how the physical body becomes insignificant. Everything we value in our lives, our selves, our families, our nation, etc., becomes subject to the spiritual person. If you are a Christian who is walking in the Spirit, then you have in reality died with Jesus and your life is hidden with Christ in God. Subsequently, persecution, insults, wrongdoings, and all other negatives that come your way will not affect you in reality.

How do you react when someone harms you or mistreats you? Are you quick to defend yourself? If so, that's one sign you may be living in the flesh.

Does it offend you when someone talks or writes negatively about your nation? If so, you are walking in the flesh. The fundamental principles Jesus taught in the spirit of love are not present in your life. The words our Lord spoke are not outmoded, neither are they invalid: "But I say unto you, Love your enemies, bless them that curse you, do good to them that hate you, and pray for them which despitefully use you, and persecute you" (Matthew 5:44).

Fanatical nationalism camouflaged in patriotism is one of the most successful tools Satan uses in the Church, particularly in the United States.

The Rebirth Process

The succession of the rebirth is described in Ephesians 1:13: "In whom ye also trusted, after that ye heard the word of truth, the gospel of your salvation: in whom also after that ye believed, ye were sealed with that holy Spirit of promise." We hear the Word of God, the Gospel of our salvation. We trust it, we believe in it...and as a result, God responds with the rebirth, which is the baptism of the Holy Spirit. Although we are still in our flesh and blood and are subject to the law of sin and death, the new person within us, born of His Spirit, is the new spiritual identity.

Our Battle Begins

Our calling as Christians is to manifest the spiritual person through our sinful flesh. But that's easier said than done.

Read how the Apostle Paul has admonished us: "Walk in the Spirit, and ye shall not fulfil the lust of the flesh. For the flesh lusteth against the Spirit, and the Spirit against the flesh: and these are contrary the one to the other: so that ye cannot do the things that ye would...But the fruit of the Spirit is love, joy, peace, longsuffering, gentleness, goodness, faith, meekness, temperance: against such there is no law. And they that are Christ's have crucified the flesh with the affections and lusts. If we live in the Spirit, let us also walk in the Spirit" (Galatians 5:16-17, 22-25).

The unbeliever does not understand Scripture and considers it foolishness. The born-again person understands Scripture through the Spirit, but in the flesh may experience difficulties in following the Spirit's instructions.

Paul's Confession

The great Apostle Paul confessed: "For that which I do I allow not: for what I would, that do I not; but what I hate, that do I...For I know that in me (that is, in my flesh,) dwelleth no good thing: for to will is present with me; but how to perform that which is good I find not. For the good that I would I do not: but the evil which I would not, that I do. Now if I do that I

70

would not, it is no more I that do it, but sin that dwelleth in me" (Romans 7:15, 18-20). Verse 24 contains the words of Paul's desperate plea: "O wretched man that I am! who shall deliver me from the body of this death?" But then Paul shows us the way to victory through Jesus Christ, and he writes down these very comforting words: "For I am persuaded, that neither death, nor life, nor angels, nor principalities, nor powers, nor things present, nor things to come, nor height, nor depth, nor any other creature, shall be able to separate us from the love of God, which is in Christ Jesus our Lord" (Romans 8:38-39).

To understand this simple but fundamental truth is vitally important for every Christian. We cannot earn our salvation or our sanctification, nor can we keep our salvation but we can know that Christ is able; His grace is sufficient.

Two-Edged Sword

What is the secret in learning to subject our flesh to the Spirit? We understand that the soul registers earthly things and the spirit heavenly things. Do they contradict each other? Indeed they do. Hebrews 4:12 explains, "For the word of God is quick, and powerful, and sharper than any two-edged sword, piercing even to the dividing asunder of soul and spirit, and of the joints and marrow, and is a discerner of the thoughts and intents of the heart." In simple terms, the more we occupy ourselves with heavenly things the less we will be bothered by earthly things. But if earthly things become the prime motivation of our lives, then we have become people who are unable to grasp the simple truths the Spirit of God attempts to convey to us.

Not only does the Word of God, the powerful two-edged sword, divide soul and spirit, the carnal from the spiritual, but it also discerns our thoughts.

Sin begins with thoughts. If we allow our thoughts to be directed by the things of this world (the flesh), then we are earth-bound, subject to gravity and unable to grasp spiritual truths. The Spirit of God must guide our thoughts so that we are spiritual people.

But there is more. Scripture includes the intents of our heart. That means thoughts we have not yet even thought of should come under the authority of the Holy Spirit. Therefore, nothing is better in the world than to occupy ourselves with the Holy Scriptures. God's Word is the dividing force between heaven and hell, light and darkness, truth and lie, spirit and soul. Therefore, choose the Holy Scripture as your ultimate guide.

Grace in Time of Need

Incidentally, only when we are spiritually exercised and have made our bodies subject to the Spirit are we able to fulfill Hebrews 4:16: "Let us therefore come boldly unto the throne of grace, that we may obtain mercy, and find grace to help in time of need." Coming before the throne of grace in prayer is not for the here and now only, but also for the future to "find grace to help in time of need." All these things belong to our preparation for our home in heaven. For that reason, we are admonished to overcome the things of this world: "He that hath an ear, let him hear what the Spirit saith unto the churches; To him that overcometh will I give to eat of the hidden manna, and will give him a white stone, and in the stone a new name written, which no man knoweth saving he that receiveth it" (Revelation 2:17).

One Way or the Other

Believers have been promised a glorious future. In contrast, the unbelievers have hope only on planet Earth: "And that no man might buy or sell, save he that had the mark, or the name of the beast, or the number of his name" (Revelation 13:17). Identifying ourselves with the Lord now is of utmost importance. No one should take a chance by playing with eternal matters. Based on Holy Scripture, there is no second chance in the everlasting eternity the believer will spend in glory and the unbeliever in suffering and pain.

There is no in-between. You are either a part of this world, which means you will receive the number of the beast or of his name, or you believe in Jesus and will receive a new name, which will result in an eternal, glorious future. Do make a decision to follow Christ today; it may be your last opportunity.

If you have grasped the deeper truth of spiritual

reality, you will also be protected from sensationalism. There is no doubt the Mark of the Beast is a sensation — actually, it's going to be a super sensation.

All of mankind — political, military, economic, religious — will be united. Deception is the only avenue that can make this unification an earthly reality. In other words, what you think is good and right may be completely wrong and evil from God's perspective. Therefore, only as a spiritual person who is walking in the Spirit, will you be put in the position to recognize the truth.

Final Deception

Let us look at one of the famous endtime chapters, Matthew 24. The disciples were impressed by what they could see, such as the temple and all the other buildings. Jesus then prophesied, "See ye not all these things? verily I say unto you, There shall not be left here one stone upon another, that shall not be thrown down" (verse 2). That was the end of the visible manifestation of the glorious temple built upon Mount Moriah in Jerusalem. The disciples wanted to know more: "Tell us, when shall these things be? and what shall be the sign of thy coming, and of the end of the world?" (verse 3). Jesus answered: "Take heed that no man deceive you." That is the key to Bible prophecy, the key also to distinguishing between the spiritual reality and physical earthly reality.

Next Jesus made this prophecy: "For many shall come in my name, saying, I am Christ; and shall deceive many. And ye shall hear of wars and rumours of wars: see that ye be not troubled: for all these things must come to pass, but the end is not yet. For nation shall rise against nation, and kingdom against kingdom: and there shall be famines, and pestilences, and earthquakes, in divers places" (verses 5-7). Note that He spoke about visible realities: wars, nations in conflict, famines, pestilences, and earthquakes. When we analyze these words in a logical manner, we conclude that He didn't prophesy anything because we always had false christs. Wars and rumors of war have not ceased from the time of Jesus until now; neither have we lacked famines, pestilences, and earthquakes. In plain words, Jesus was saying, the time as it is now will continue. He didn't say there will be an increase in wars, or more famines, pestilences and earthquakes.

Unfortunately, many have written about this subject claiming that today there are more wars, pestilences and earthquakes. But the opposite is actually true: we have fewer wars, fewer famines and fewer pestilences. It is extremely short-sighted to point to some military conflict and say it fulfills the prophecy that "there shall be wars and rumors of wars." Each time exceptional natural catastrophes take place, many believers label these events in the attempt to prove that particular prophecy. But as we have just seen, there is no prophetic content whatsoever. We always have had and always will have earthquakes, pestilences, famines and wars.

However, the decrease is certainly a shadow of things to come, namely world peace. Therefore, the Apostle Paul warned: "For when they shall say, Peace and safety; then sudden destruction cometh upon them, as travail upon a woman with child; and they shall not escape" (1 Thessalonians 5:3).

We have an indirect prophecy in the calamities Jesus speaks about, for they seemingly begin to disappear through political negotiation and scientific discovery, thereby deceiving mankind. Nevertheless, the future for the world looks bleak. The problems of the world will seemingly be solved, but from a spiritual perspective we know it's only the deception of the grand master, the great deceiver, the father of lies, the devil himself. Peter summarized the future with these words:

> Seeing then that all these things shall be dissolved, what manner of persons ought ye to be in all holy conversation and godliness, Looking for and hasting unto the coming of the day of God, wherein the heavens being on fire shall be dissolved, and the elements shall melt with fervent heat? Nevertheless we, according to his promise, look for new heavens and a new earth, wherein dwelleth righteousness. Wherefore, beloved, seeing that ye look for such things, be diligent that ye may be found of him in peace, without spot, and blameless (2 Peter 3:11-14).

Chapter 5

NOT THE MARK OF THE BEAST

Before we go any further on this subject, let's first identify some of the so-called marks of the beast which we believe have no direct relationship to the fulfillment of Revelation 13:16-17.

I came up with more than two million hits when I typed in the words "Mark of the Beast" in the Yahoo search engine. Thus, there are endless ideas about the Mark of the Beast, what it is, how it will be applied, and the technology that will be implemented. An overwhelming amount of information is available regarding the numerous theories surrounding the Mark of the Beast. Therefore, if you have read this book thus far and hoped to find details about the actual physical Mark of the Beast, I am sorry to disappoint you. Quite simply, the Mark of the Beast and the image of the beast are prophetic entities that come with no further details attached. Subsequently, we will look in vain to identify anything today that could potentially be used as the Mark of the Beast.

Nevertheless, much scientific development points to the eventual implementation of the Mark of the Beast.

Implanted Chip

The most popular theory explaining how the Mark of the Beast will be executed is the implanted chip.

One of the most celebrated implant systems is the VeriChip *(http://www.adsx.com/prodserpart/verichip.html)*:

> An implantable, radio frequency identification biochip slightly larger than the size of a grain of rice, can be scanned (using equipment expected to cost between $1,000 and $3,000) to give a unique ID number. Its use is touted for security and emergency, as well as for medical applications. In South America, the chip has been bundled with a GPS-unit and sold to potential kidnap victims, *Wired* (http://wired.com/news/technology/0,1282,51575,00.html) reports.

The article also speaks about the medical purposes for the chip:

> In medicine (the main market), the idea is that if a patient is unconscious or otherwise unable to tell doctors about medical conditions then doctors can still find out this information from the ID contained on the VeriChip. This number is ...cross-referenced with hospital databases to give a patient's medical records.
>
> It seems little more convenient than if a person

is say, diabetic or has a rare blood group, or has an allergy, and carries this information by an unbreakable bracelet around their wrist. Judging from its web site, Applied Digital Solutions is a little more ambitious: it appears to want to store medical information on the chip.

Another article states:

It's the ultimate status symbol for celebrities — a $5,000 chip inside their bodies that can track them down by satellite anywhere on the earth. The 4mm by 4mm chip has a deadly serious purpose: to ensure that the victim of a kidnap can be found wherever they are hidden. According to the UK *Sunday Times,* Israeli company Gen-Etics makes the chip based on technology developed by the secret service Mossad. So far 43 Europeans and Americans have had the chip inserted under their skin (*Looksmart,* 14 October 1998).

Obviously, this is not the latest news. In fact, it's old. While I'm writing these lines or when you are reading them, much more is developing in the field of computer science and personal identification. At this time, therefore, we again confirm what is written in Scripture: the Mark of the Beast will be applied on the right hand or on the forehead of every person on earth; otherwise, a person will not be able to live. Please keep these facts in mind when you read this or any other prophetic literature: the Word of God will be fulfilled in its finest detail, but how precisely and at what time exactly we do not know. Thus again, spiritual matters must be discerned spiritually and for that reason, the prophetic Word, particularly in the book of Revelation, concludes: "He that hath an ear to hear, let him hear what the Spirit saith unto the churches" (Revelation 2:17).

Ancient Technology

In computer terminology, these things are actually "ancient" technology. Computer technology is developing at such a fast pace that inventions older than a year are already considered obsolete.

Meanwhile, many more countries are selling this type of security system and needless to say, with each new day, something better, faster and more accurate comes along.

Therefore, I venture to say that this chip is not the Mark of the Beast. However, I must allow that this technology is part of the preparation toward the Mark of the Beast.

What is important to realize is that according to Scripture, the Mark of the Beast comes in conjunction with the man-made image of the beast. That means a manufactured item will be able to recognize who "would not worship the image of the beast." Therefore, the Mark of the Beast must not be limited to a passive storage of data, but must be capable of dispensing data as well.

Future Technology

A number of books line my bookshelf with fascinating titles such as *Engines of Tomorrow* or *When Things Start To Think*. These books deal with modern inventions that are shaping our world. Intelligent and educated scientists try to push the envelope a little further into the future almost daily.

The following statement is found in the inside cover of the book *When Things Start To Think:* "We live in a world of increasingly intrusive information technology, requiring that people meet the needs of machines rather than the other way around." The author, Mr. Neil Gershenfeld, "shows how to dismantle the barrier between the bits of the digital world and the atoms of our physical world in order to bring together the best attributes of both worlds." The book description concludes: "This is a book for people who want to know what the future is going to look like — and for people who want to know how to create the future."

It becomes clear, after reading just a few chapters, that the implanted chip is "stone age technology." We have advanced much further than we may think.

Chapter 6

THE MARK OF THE BEAST

And I beheld another beast coming up out of the earth; and he had two horns like a lamb, and he spake as a dragon. And he exerciseth all the power of the first beast before him, and causeth the earth and them which dwell therein to worship the first beast, whose deadly wound was healed. And he doeth great wonders, so that he maketh fire come down from heaven on the earth in the sight of men, And deceiveth them that dwell on the earth by the means of those miracles which he had power to do in the sight of the beast; saying to them that dwell on the earth, that they should make an image to the beast, which had the wound by a sword, and did live. And he had power to give life unto the image of the beast, that the image of the beast should both speak, and cause that as many as would not worship the image of the beast should be killed. And he causeth all, both small and great, rich and poor, free and bond, to receive a mark in their right hand, or in their foreheads: And that no man might buy or sell, save he that had the mark, or the name of the beast, or the number of his name. Here is wisdom. Let him that hath understanding count the number of the beast: for it is the number of a man; and his number is Six hundred threescore and six (Revelation 13:11-18).

The above seven verses make up a compact prophecy that describes how the world will experience a truly global political and economic system, supported by a unified world religious faith, enforced by "another beast." This other beast demonstrates his authority by producing "great wonders" and "miracles."

The crowning achievement will be the implementation of a global registration system of all people, coupled with a perfectly controlled economy, and all that to secure the rule of the first beast: the Antichrist.

The Well Known Mark of the Beast

I typed the words "Mark of the Beast" in the search engine of my internet provider and came up with the following results:

MSN Search - 444,934
Ask Jeeves - 647,700
Google - 1,020,000
Alta Vista - 2,280,000
Yahoo - 2,310,000

These listings confirm that the phrase "mark of the beast" is a common phrase that the public is very well acquainted with.

To research the meaning of the phrase according to the listings from these search engines would be a mindboggling undertaking, and I believe of little, if any, help.

In general, however, the key words within the phrase "Mark of the Beast" point to Revelation 13 and clearly refer to a political, religious, military, economic and commercial system that will be global.

The Bible Facts

To attain a more complete picture of the Mark of the Beast, let us also read Revelation 13:1-10:

> And I stood upon the sand of the sea, and saw a beast rise up out of the sea, having seven heads and ten horns, and upon his horns ten crowns, and upon his heads the name of blasphemy. And the beast which I saw was like unto a leopard, and his feet were as the feet of a bear, and his mouth as the mouth of a lion: and the dragon gave him his power, and his seat, and great authority. And I saw one of his heads as it were wounded to death; and his deadly wound was healed: and all the world wondered after the beast. And they worshipped the dragon which gave power unto the beast: and they worshipped the beast, saying, Who is like unto the beast? who is able to make war with him? And there was given unto him a mouth speaking

great things and blasphemies; and power was given unto him to continue forty and two months. And he opened his mouth in blasphemy against God, to blaspheme his name, and his tabernacle, and them that dwell in heaven. And it was given unto him to make war with the saints, and to overcome them: and power was given him over all kindreds, and tongues, and nations. And all that dwell upon the earth shall worship him, whose names are not written in the book of life of the Lamb slain from the foundation of the world. If any man have an ear, let him hear. He that leadeth into captivity shall go into captivity: he that killeth with the sword must be killed with the sword. Here is the patience and the faith of the saints.

In short, that is the preparation for the implementation of the Mark of the Beast.

The Beast: Spiritual or Physical?

When we read the first three verses of Revelation 13, we may identify this beast as a spiritual entity unknown to us on earth. No such animal on earth looks like a leopard, a bear and a lion. To understand what John writes about, we must point out that he was in heaven, so he was seeing things from a heavenly perspective. Thus, the identity of the first beast up to this point is demonic and not physical.

However, verses 3-4 make it clear that this beast is also a physical identity on earth. In other words, John was describing what was happening in heaven, and what simultaneously transpires on earth. This also is emphasized in verse 4, where the people on earth offer great praises and even worship the beast.

Furthermore, the beast blasphemes God and those who "dwell in heaven." The beast therefore is now on earth. Also, to make war with the saints is not possible if they are in heaven, so they must be on earth. The people of the world are identified with the words "kindred," "tongues" and "nations."

Then in verse 8 that all who live upon the earth will worship him. Thus, we are dealing with a man who happens to be the epitome of evil on earth. There is no way we can spiritualize this fact with the conclusion that the beast is a spiritual, demonic being without a physical identity.

The same is true of the second beast, or "another beast," as he is identified in verse 11. While verse 11 does reveal a demonic entity, because no one runs around with two horns on his head, we see in verses 12-16 that this is a person, another manifestation of evil, but in the form of man. Notice the word "earth." Thus, his power is earthly, it's real, it's physical. Later in Revelation 19:20, we read: "These both [beasts 1 and 2] were cast alive into a lake of fire burning with brimstone." Therefore we can say with assurance that the Antichrist and the false prophet are real people who have been empowered by Satan, and whose specific task is to deceive mankind.

The First Beast

The first beast comes from out of the sea. It is generally agreed that the sea represents the nations of the world. This beast is a person who is being ordained and empowered by the dragon, whom Scripture identifies as the "old serpent," the "devil," and "Satan."

It may be helpful to take a closer look at the various names used to identify the evil one: "the great dragon," "old serpent," "devil," and "Satan." The word "dragon" is only used in the book of Revelation and depicts a gigantic power superceding that of a human. The "serpent" played a key role in the deception of Adam and Eve. A serpent is cunning, fast and often deadly. The English word "devil" comes from the Greek word *diabolos,* which means "accuser." He is a slanderer, the father of lies, and a murderer from the beginning. Satan is the chief of the fallen spirits. *Unger's Bible Dictionary* defines the word by using various titles: "Satan is also called the *Devil,* the *Dragon,* the *Evil One,* the *Angel of the Bottomless Pit,* the *Prince of this World,* the *Prince of the Power of the Air,* the *God of this World,* Apollyon, Abaddon, Belial, Bellzebub" (pg. 972).

We also learned that "all the world" admires this beast to such an extent that the people actually worship him and the dragon who gave power and authority to the beast.

From the statement, "who is like unto the beast, who is able to make war with him?" it becomes clear that he is also a great military leader, for no one can oppose him with weapons of war. He is the supreme ruler, the great benevolent leader whom all people will love, admire and worship. A special characteristic of this beast is that he blasphemes God, and even destroys the saints of God.

It is important to point out that this first beast receives everything from the dragon: "The dragon gave him his power, and his seat, and great authority" (Revelation 13:2). Then in verse 4 we read: "And they worshipped the dragon which gave power unto the beast." And furthermore, in verse 5 we read: "And there was given unto him a mouth speaking great things and blasphemies; and power was given unto him to continue forty and two months." Then verse 7 explains: "And it was given unto him to make war with the saints, and to overcome them: and power was given him over all kindreds, and tongues, and nations."

It is evident from these few Scriptures that the beast that comes from out of the sea having ten heads and ten crowns is apparently an unknown, powerless identity by himself and has nothing in his own right. In other words, he is a nobody whom Satan sets up to be his right-hand man. Doubtless, he will possess all of the characteristics necessary to appeal to endtime Churchianity and to the rest of the world. He will be able to unite all people, and therefore all people will praise, worship and adore him.

The Second Beast

There is a distinct difference between the first beast, which comes from out of the sea, and the second beast, which comes from out of the earth. Unlike the first beast, who receives everything from Satan, the second beast apparently possesses all power in his own right.

Let's look at a few examples from Scripture:

- "he had two horns like a lamb" (verse 11)
- "he exerciseth all the power" (verse 12)
- "he doeth great wonders (verse 13)
- "he maketh fire come down from heaven" (verse 13)
- "he deceiveth them that dwell on the earth" (verse 14)
- "he had power" (verse 14)
- "he had power" (verse 15).

The second beast possesses all power and uses it to promote the first beast.

This man will actually perform miracles: "he maketh fire come down from heaven on the earth in the sight of men" (verse 13). Here we see mankind's desire — "I only believe what I see" being fulfilled. Unbelievers will now be able to see, can believe and therefore wholeheartedly follow the advice of the second beast to be actively involved in building this glorious, peaceful and benevolent society. This will be true democracy in action. The overwhelming majority of the world's population will realize that this man has the ability to unite the world and enforce law and order for all people. Finally, this will be a man according to the heart of men, one they can all trust.

The Image

Here are the instructions given to the world by the second beast: "they should make an image to the beast." Our imaginations tend to run wild when we consider what makes up this "image of the beast." We do know, however, that this manufactured image of the beast does not come from heaven, nor does it come from hell, but it is a man-made object produced by people who dwell on the earth.

Give Life Unto the Image

Next, the second beast does something unprecedented in human history: he gives life to the image of the beast. Something made by man becomes alive. What this "life" consists of becomes evident in the activity of the image of the beast, who now can do two things: speak and "cause that as many as would not worship the image of the beast should be killed" (verse 15). Now the image of the beast is capable of discerning who worships him and who does not. And, the image has the authority to impose capital punishment against those who do not worship the image.

All enemies will be eliminated when this system is implemented. The dream of most people is now becoming a reality: eradication of all opposition.

Think about the benefit the people of the world would reap: there would be no more terrorism. There wouldn't be any more terrorists because the image of the beast would have the ability to identify and eliminate the perpetrators. That would be one significant reason for the world to unite more than ever before.

Surely politicians wish they didn't have any opposition so that they could implement their own policies and ideas. I am quite sure that there are many in the United States who wish there weren't any opposition to the prevailing government. In effect, they actually desire a one-party system, which is simply the beginning of a global democratic dictatorship. The time will come when democracy and religion are united and it will be virtually impossible to exist without worshipping the image of the beast, as we will see later.

The next step is total economic control. You will not be able to go to the mall, eat at a restaurant, fill your gas tank, pay your utility bills or make your mortgage payment without the Mark of the Beast. You will have to submit to the economic, financial, political and religious system in accordance with the desires and plans of the second beast. Total control will and must be implemented.

According to the facts documented in Scripture, we can be absolutely certain that these things will come to pass globally. We do not know how they will be implemented, or when this process will begin, but we do know that preparations are in full swing right this minute.

Revelation 13 contains information we have briefly analyzed, by which we can conclude that total control cannot allow itself any opposition. There *will* be a one-world ruler. Religion *will* become unified. Only one significant military power *will* exist. Global economy with total control *will* be implemented. These are biblically documented facts. We don't need to debate the issue or question these statements. We believe in the absolute truth of the prophecies contained in the Bible. "And he causeth all, both small and great, rich and poor, free and bond, to receive a mark in their right hand, or in their foreheads: And that no man might buy or sell, save he that had the mark, or the name of the beast, or the number of his name" (Revelation 13:16-17). That, we can say, is the ultimate victory of the evil one.

Chapter 7

GOD'S IDENTITY SYSTEM

The title of this chapter may be misunderstood by some readers, and therefore I must explain. God does not need any system, at least not one based on our understanding. He is sovereign, omnipotent, omniscient, and omnipresent, and He isn't bound by our fickle definitions. In this chapter we will look at what is taking place in the invisible world, and at Satan's attempt to mimic God.

Let's first read about His very personal interest in His people, Israel: "But now thus saith the LORD that created thee, O Jacob, and he that formed thee, O Israel, Fear not: for I have redeemed thee, I have called thee by thy name; thou art mine" (Isaiah 43:1). He knows Jacob and Israel and He knows the name because He is the originator, the Creator of man and earth.

What a great comfort this is for us during our trials and tribulations. We may be nothing in this world but a number, but when we are born again of the

Spirit of God, He knows us — He even knows you by your name. Let that comfort you, strengthen your faith, and give you the assurance that you belong to Him.

Adam

"This is the book of the generations of Adam. In the day that God created man, in the likeness of God made he him; Male and female created he them; and blessed them, and called their name Adam, in the day when they were created" (Genesis 5:1-2).

God identified the first two people on planet Earth by one name: Adam. This word, in the Hebrew, means "ground" or "red ground." Man has been created from the substance of the ground. "And the LORD God formed man of the dust of the ground, and breathed into his nostrils the breath of life; and man became a living soul" (Genesis 2:7). We read God's judgment of man's sin in Genesis 3:19: "In the sweat of thy face shalt thou eat bread, till thou return unto the ground; for out of it wast thou taken: for dust thou art, and unto dust shalt thou return."

Adam was separated from God from that point forward. Previously, the two represented the perfect unity of God, expressed in God the Father, God the Son and God the Holy Spirit.

After the Fall, "Adam called his wife's name Eve; because she was the mother of all living" (Genesis 3:20). Separation had taken place.

We must pause here for a minute, and realize that

God's intention is expressed in perfect union. Therefore, division and separation are not part of God's original intention. From one identity, Adam became two: Adam and Eve.

Genesis Chapter 5 outlines the genealogy of mankind, from Adam to Noah. Noah means "rest" or "being quiet." Noah and his family were saved from the flood. The world was populated by the descendants of Noah and his three sons.

Luke Chapter 4 provides the genealogy of Jesus, tracking His line through Joseph and Adam. The meaning of each name in the genealogy carries prophetic significance. That, doubtless, is God's identity system; He only creates originals, for He is the only Creator. Each person is unique, which is a testimony to God's creative power.

Although tremendous progress had been made regarding the intricacies of a person's identity, especially in such areas as fingerprints, blood samples and DNA, I do not believe man has yet discovered anything worth mentioning when compared with the knowledge of the Creator. Remember, God's ways are beyond finding out; His wisdom is inexhaustible.

The One and Only God

It is important to point out that God is very personal with His children. Many times in Scripture we read "God of Israel." But that does not necessarily mean Israel collectively, as a nation, because Israel was also a person whose name was changed from

Jacob. Jacob made this clear when he prayed to God; thus, we read in Genesis 28:13: "And, behold, the LORD stood above it, and said, I am the LORD God of Abraham thy father, and the God of Isaac: the land whereon thou liest, to thee will I give it, and to thy seed." He didn't say "the God of Abraham and Isaac," but the "God of Abraham...and the God of Isaac." In Genesis 49:24, we read: "and the arms of his hands were made strong by the hands of the mighty God of Jacob; (from thence is the shepherd, the stone of Israel)."

We do well to remember these important facts when we deal with the subject of God's identity system. Nothing is systematic about it; it is very individual and intimate.

The New Name

Let's look at five examples in the book of Revelation where names are mentioned:

• "He that hath an ear, let him hear what the Spirit saith unto the churches; To him that overcometh will I give to eat of the hidden manna, and will give him a white stone, and in the stone a new name written, which no man knoweth saving he that receiveth it" (Revelation 2:17).

• "Him that overcometh will I make a pillar in the temple of my God, and he shall go no more out: and I will write upon him the name of my God, and the name of the city of my God, which is new Jerusalem, which cometh down out of heaven from my God: and

I will write upon him my new name" (Revelation 3:12).

• "And I looked, and, lo, a Lamb stood on the mount Sion, and with him an hundred forty and four thousand, having his Father's name written in their foreheads" (Revelation 14:1).

• "His eyes were as a flame of fire, and on his head were many crowns; and he had a name written, that no man knew, but he himself" (Revelation 19:12).

• "And they shall see his face; and his name shall be in their foreheads" (Revelation 22:4).

God identified His chosen people with a name, not a number. That is the difference between the work of God and the work of Satan.

In this case, Scripture does not contain any additional information that would reveal what this new name is, how it is applied, or whether it is visible. What is revealed, however, is that this name is very personal: "No man knoweth saving he that received it." Even the Lord Himself has a name that "no man knew but he himself."

Here is a deep mystery on a spiritual level that we cannot fully fathom other than to realize that God is very intimately concerned about each one of us.

We, too, have our little secrets. For example, husbands and wives often have their own intimate language that no one else understands; it's very personal and is not to be shared with anyone else.

The real depth of what is to come and how it actually relates to this hidden name belongs to the unsearchable riches of God.

First Peter 1:12 states: "Unto whom it was revealed, that not unto themselves, but unto us they did minister the things, which are now reported unto you by them that have preached the gospel unto you with the Holy Ghost sent down from heaven; which things the angels desire to look into." These things have even been hidden from the angels.

We must add 1 Corinthians 2:9-10: "But as it is written, Eye hath not seen, nor ear heard, neither have entered into the heart of man, the things which God hath prepared for them that love him. But God hath revealed them unto us by his Spirit: for the Spirit searcheth all things, yea, the deep things of God." That means we cannot use our intellect or imagination to grasp what God has prepared for us. We can only comprehend it in our spirit. A constant and closer walk with the Lord will open up the unseen riches that God has prepared for you and for me.

Legion of Demons

To better understand what is taking place in the invisible world, particularly relating to our theme of "God's Identity System," we must look at an event that took place during Jesus' time.

When Jesus entered the land of Gadarenes, He was met by a demon-possessed person who immediately identified Him: "What have I to do with thee, Jesus, thou Son of the most high God? I adjure thee by God, that thou torment me not" (Mark 5:7). (Incidentally, this proves that the devil and his demons know they have been given only a limited span of time.)

The demon pleaded: "torment me not," which reveals the demons also know that the lake of fire will be their ultimate destiny: "the devil that deceived them was cast into the lake of fire and brimstone, where the beast and the false prophet are, and shall be tormented day and night for ever and ever" (Revelation 20:10).

Jesus did two things: He commanded the spirit to "Come out of the man, thou unclean spirit" (verse 8) and then He asked: "What is thy name?" Verse 9 reveals the answer: "My name is Legion: for we are many." It is typical of the devil to make a general statement about himself and not reveal the exact name. According to Roman history, a legion could consist of 6,000 or 12,500 soldiers. Therefore, the devil, the lord of the demons, gives only a vague answer; "we are a legion," a number.

Typically, Satan is more interested in numbers by which he can confuse and deceive countless people on earth.

Holiness to the Lord

Exodus 39:30 provides another illustration of how God shows His intention for His people: "And they made the plate of the holy crown of pure gold, and wrote upon it a writing, like to the engravings of a signet, HOLINESS TO THE LORD." This is God's plan for you, too. He has saved us based on the shed blood of His beloved Son, the Lord Jesus Christ, in order to place this sign on your forehead: "Holiness to the Lord." That is our calling.

We have been called to live a life that is holy and separated from this world. We have been ordained to be lights in this world and salt on this earth, not to glorify ourselves. Ephesians 1:4 states: "According as he hath chosen us in him before the foundation of the world, that we should be holy and without blame before him in love." What is the purpose of our being chosen? "To the praise of the glory of his grace" (verse 6).

Think about it for a moment: We have been chosen to be something, "To the praise of the glory of his grace." Please don't confuse your physical appearance or position with your spiritual one. Our bodies of flesh and blood are subject to sin, sickness and death. But that which has been born within you through the Spirit of God is the real you. It is His work for the "praise of the glory of his grace."

His Work to His Glory

Another example may be appropriate. Consider a painter. Many people admire great works of art, and may stand in line for hours just to see certain exhibits. Others will pay great sums of money to buy a piece of art. These works of art don't receive the glory themselves; they glorify their maker. The value of the painting reflects the talent and skill of the artist.

There are millions of great paintings in the world, but when a picture is discovered to have been painted by a well-known artist, it becomes worth a lot of money — not because of the painting itself, but because of the painter.

This is an important concept in our spiritual lives. Perhaps you are physically unattractive, or don't believe you have achieved much. Maybe you never were a part of the popular clique, or you may be suffering from an illness that makes life a daily battle. You would be greatly mistaken to think that your appearance, position or circumstances have anything to do with your spiritual identity. The real you is the new person who has been created through the Spirit of God. God created you to give praise of His glory.

Losers' Fellowship

The Apostle Paul wrote these words in his first letter to the church at Corinth after God saved him: "For ye see your calling, brethren, how that not many wise men after the flesh, not many mighty, not many noble, are called: But God hath chosen the foolish things of the world to confound the wise; and God hath chosen the weak things of the world to confound the things which are mighty. And base things of the world, and things which are despised, hath God chosen, yea, and things which are not, to bring to nought things that are" (1 Corinthians 1:26-28). Do you want to be a part of this group of people who are considered foolish, weak, base, and despised?

103

It is unfortunate that in modern Churchianity, even within certain Bible-believing Christian circles, the outward person is pampered, honored and glorified. We don't hear many messages on how to become weak and despised. Who wants to be rejected? No one! Yet we are admonished in Scripture to follow Jesus, the Man described by the prophet Isaiah as: "despised and rejected of men; a man of sorrows, and acquainted with grief: and we hid as it were our faces from him; he was despised, and we esteemed him not" (Isaiah 53:3). Jesus is described as being despised, rejected, a man of sorrows, acquainted with grief and not esteemed.

Can you imagine a ministry calling itself the "Church of the Despised?" Or "The Ministry of the Rejected?" Today's ministries and churches take great pains to come across as positive, as offering various ways to improve yourself, or as presenting strategies to be a member of the winning team. A church with a name like "Loser's Fellowship" probably would not have people lined up outside the door waiting to come in!

Is Your Faith Real?

With these few questions we are starting to uncover a sore point that concerns believers. We are no more than what the Bible says. We are not the glorious, victorious, conquering church, filled with good health, wealth and happiness. We are the little flock that is despised, rejected, persecuted and occasionally even killed. That is the true Church, the Body of Christ, the Bride of the Lamb. If you realize that, then you belong to the true Church. But if your inner being rebels against those thoughts, then you must ask yourself: Am I really a part of the Body of Christ? Have I been born again of His Spirit or have I been deceived by another spirit?

Is there even such a thing as another spirit? Not only is there another spirit, but there is another Jesus and another gospel as well. This is documented in 2 Corinthians 11:4: "For if he that cometh preacheth another Jesus, whom we have not preached, or if ye receive another spirit, which ye have not received, or another gospel, which ye have not accepted, ye might well bear with him." Quite frankly, I fear for the many millions of precious souls who have been lulled into a false sense of security and who believe they are saved, but who have no idea who the Jesus of the Bible is.

The Fruit of the Spirit

Matthew 7 contains a description of a group of people who call Jesus "Lord," who testify of the great things they have done in the name of Jesus, and who have even prophesied. Here is the simple truth: "Wherefore by their fruits ye shall know them. Not every one that saith unto me, Lord, Lord, shall enter into the kingdom of heaven; but he that doeth the will of my Father which is in heaven. Many will say to me in that day, Lord, Lord, have we not prophesied in thy name? and in thy name have cast out devils? and in thy name done many wonderful works? And then will I profess unto them, I never knew you: depart from me, ye that work iniquity" (Matthew 7:20-23). We must stress that these people are not unbelievers (atheists), neither are they Muslims or Hindus; these people are very close to our camp because they call Jesus "Lord."

The Lord seemed to be rather cruel when He opposed these hard-working, diligent, faithful servants who apparently had done everything in His Name. He said, "Depart from me ye that work iniquity."

Why did He say that? Simply because they bore no spiritual fruit even though they obviously possessed spiritual gifts. But the key is "fruit," not "gifts": "ye shall know them by their fruits."

This fruit is described in Galatians 5:22-23: "But the fruit of the Spirit is love, joy, peace, longsuffering, gentleness, goodness, faith, meekness, temperance: against such there is no law." Of course, the fruit of the Spirit may be imitated, but it doesn't last long. All of the attributes listed in Galatians 5:22-23 will turn bad if not genuine. If the fruit of the Spirit has been created by God Himself, then the one who follows Jesus will willingly and deliberately crucify his flesh. Galatians 5:24 describes such believers with these words: "they that are Christ's have crucified the flesh with the affections and lusts."

Does Jesus Know *You?*

The key words in Christ's rejection of these alleged followers is expressed in the words "I never knew you." Therefore, whether or not Jesus knows you is significant. I'm not asking whether you know Jesus, but whether Jesus knows *you.* Your answer bears eternal consequences.

There is a picture hanging in my office of Ariel Sharon and me shaking hands, smiling broadly as if we had known each other for years. Ariel Sharon was not prime minister at that time; he had appeared as a featured speaker at our conference in Jerusalem and I was the interpreter. I knew him; I wouldn't have a problem picking Ariel Sharon out of a great crowd. But if you had asked him if he knew me, I'm sure he would have answered "no."

You Must Be Family

How can we be certain the Lord knows us? The answer is simple: We must belong to the family of God. Family members cultivate intimate relationships with one another. The President of the United States knows his family, his relatives, his close friends and his staff, but he doesn't know the rest of us. But Jesus knows everyone by name. Anyone who comes to Him in true repentance and humility, asking forgiveness for sin, becomes a child of God.

That process is clearly described in Ephesians 1:13: "In whom ye also trusted, after that ye heard the word of truth, the gospel of your salvation: in whom

107

also after that ye believed, ye were sealed with that holy Spirit of promise." You are a child of God for all eternity from that point on. Jesus knows you by name.

Does that mean Jesus has no knowledge or recognition of people outside of the family of God? Of course He does. He knows *all* men. In fact, the Bible says He knows what's *inside* every person. But for this discussion, we are concerned with the new person, not the one born of flesh and blood, which is subject to this earth. The one born of spirit and water, the eternal person, formed by the Holy Spirit into the image of the Beloved is what counts.

Flesh and Spirit

What happens when we become new creatures in Christ? Second Corinthians 5:17 answers: "Therefore if any man be in Christ, he is a new creature: old things are passed away; behold, all things are become new." What does it mean to be a new creature? What things have passed away? What things have become new? We are making a great mistake if we think that our old nature has been renewed and that our flesh has been sanctified.

Let's read verse 15: "And that he died for all, that they which live should not henceforth live unto themselves, but unto him which died for them, and rose again." Thus, the new creation depends on the death of the old creature. We no longer live for ourselves, because we have died with Christ. The Apostle Paul made it clear that he was speaking of two different people: one of flesh and blood and the other born of the Spirit. The one made of flesh and blood represents sin; it must be crucified, and must die in Christ. Our physical bodies do not have the same promise as the spiritual person.

When the Apostle Paul wrote about dying in Christ and no longer living in the flesh, he also wrote: "Wherefore henceforth know we no man after the flesh: yea, though we have known Christ after the flesh, yet now henceforth know we him no more" (2 Corinthians 5:16). Here is a serious word about the confusion between the spiritual person and the one that has been born of flesh and blood. Although we are still alive, the Apostle Paul says he does not know anyone "after the flesh." He goes even further, because he saw Christ in the flesh; nevertheless, he wrote: "henceforth know we him no more." In other words, "it is of no advantage to me to have seen Christ in the flesh, it did not sanctify me more, reinforce my salvation deeper or benefit me in any way, shape or form spiritually."

We have emphasized the absolute necessity of the rebirth with its consequences to show that there is no other way to become a part of God's identity system than through Jesus Christ our Lord. He already has each of us identified by a new name, but one day you will know, for it is written: "no man knoweth saveth he that receiveth it."

Do we now understand why Jesus told these people He didn't know them? They came to Him in their flesh, but they were not recognized as being born-again children of God. They did not belong to the family of God; thus, they would be lost for all eternity.

This group of people Jesus said He never knew were deceived. As a result, they will gladly accept the Mark of the Beast, and will believe that peace has come to earth. Man finally will have accomplished his age-old desire to usher in peace on earth and good will to man, but it is all a deception because it will lead to the greatest catastrophe the world has ever known.

You must decide to become part of the group that has been transformed into the image of the Beloved via the way of the cross — that is, to be rejected, to suffer, to become despised and to die. The alternative is to belong to the successful, self-confident, and hard-working people who proudly present their case to the Lord, yet who ultimately will be rejected by Him: "I never knew you: depart from me, ye that work iniquity" (Matthew 7:23).

Time is short; the return of Christ is near, and the moment of truth is not far away. But for you, it may be the last opportunity to say yes to the real Jesus, the suffering Servant who invites you to take up your cross and follow Him.

Chapter 8

WAR IN HEAVEN

Now it's time to take another look at Lucifer, who is the reason for all the turmoil that takes place both in the invisible world and visible one. Revelation Chapter 12 explains how the devil got to earth:

> And there appeared a great wonder in heaven; a woman clothed with the sun, and the moon under her feet, and upon her head a crown of twelve stars: And she being with child cried, travailing in birth, and pained to be delivered. And there appeared another wonder in heaven; and behold a great red dragon, having seven heads and ten horns, and seven crowns upon his heads. And his tail drew the third part of the stars of heaven, and did cast them to the earth: and the dragon stood before the woman which was ready to be delivered, for to devour her child as soon as it was born. And she brought forth a man child, who was to rule all nations with a rod of iron: and

111

her child was caught up unto God, and to his throne. And the woman fled into the wilderness, where she hath a place prepared of God, that they should feed her there a thousand two hundred and threescore days. And there was war in heaven: Michael and his angels fought against the dragon; and the dragon fought and his angels, And prevailed not; neither was their place found any more in heaven. And the great dragon was cast out, that old serpent, called the Devil, and Satan, which deceiveth the whole world: he was cast out into the earth, and his angels were cast out with him. And I heard a loud voice saying in heaven, Now is come salvation, and strength, and the kingdom of our God, and the power of his Christ: for the accuser of our brethren is cast down, which accused them before our God day and night. And they overcame him by the blood of the Lamb, and by the word of their testimony; and they loved not their lives unto the death. Therefore rejoice, ye heavens, and ye that dwell in them. Woe to the inhabitants of the earth and of the sea! for the devil is come down unto you, having great wrath, because he knoweth that he hath but a short time. And when the dragon saw that he was cast unto the earth, he persecuted the woman which brought forth the man child. And to the woman were given two wings of a great eagle, that she might fly into the wilderness, into her place, where she is nourished for a time, and times, and half a time, from the face of the serpent. And the serpent cast out of his mouth water as a flood after the woman, that he might cause her to be carried away of the flood. And the earth helped the woman, and the earth opened her mouth, and swallowed up the flood which the dragon cast out of his mouth. And the dragon was wroth with the woman, and went to make war with the remnant of her seed, which keep the commandments of God, and have the testimony of Jesus Christ (Revelation 12).

This event is taking place in heaven. Therefore, we must not make the mistake of trying to analyze it from an earthly perspective. We are very limited in our understanding of heavenly things. John, however, was raptured into heaven and from there he reported: "After this I looked, and, behold, a door was opened in heaven: and the first voice which I heard was as it were of a trumpet talking with me; which said, Come up hither, and I will shew thee things which must be hereafter. And immediately I was in the spirit: and, behold, a throne was set in heaven, and one sat on the throne" (Revelation 4:1-2). He reported what he saw from eternity, that is, from a heavenly perspective.

Scripture explains that God is from everlasting to everlasting; He is the beginning and the end. The Bible states that, in the end, time as we know it will no longer exist, because eternity will take over. John saw and reported events from the past, present and future, all compacted into one.

Heavenly Confrontation

What does that mean to us? When John saw the events in heaven he saw what had transpired in history as if they were taking place in the present. He saw events that would be fulfilled thousands of years later as if they already had been accomplished.

For example, consider Revelation 13:8b: "the Lamb slain from the foundation of the world." The Lamb was slain about 2,000 years ago outside the walls of Jerusalem on Calvary's cross, and not at an earlier date when the foundation of the world had been laid. But here we see that the past and the future cease to exist, because they are viewed from a heavenly perspective.

Let's look at a further example: "And hath raised us up together, and made us sit together in heavenly places in Christ Jesus" (Ephesians 2:6). Obviously we have not been "raised up" because we are still on earth. But from a heavenly vantage, that has already been accomplished; we are spiritually in His presence "together in heavenly places in Christ Jesus."

Philippians 3:20 also refers to eternal things: "For our conversation is in heaven; from whence also we look for the Saviour, the Lord Jesus Christ." Again, this doesn't sound right to those of us reading these words, because we are on earth and not in heaven. And it is from the earth that we look to the sky expecting the Lord to return. But it becomes a different story from a heavenly perspective. Our conversation already "is in heaven," and from that heavenly

114

position we look for our Savior, the Lord Jesus Christ.

The Woman Clothed With the Sun

Back to Revelation Chapter 12. This woman is not an actual flesh-and-blood person. How do we know? Because Scripture says she is "clothed with the sun." Obviously that is impossible. Even if the earth moved only a few kilometers closer to the sun, everything on earth would be incinerated. Thus, we must learn to view this from a spiritual perspective: this "woman" is about to bring forth the man-child, who will "rule all nations with a rod of iron."

To understand this we need to analyze it from the opposite angle: Who will rule all nations with a rod of iron? The Lord Jesus Christ. A closer description is found in Revelation 19:12-16:

> His eyes were as a flame of fire, and on his head were many crowns; and he had a name written, that no man knew, but he himself. And he was clothed with a vesture dipped in blood: and his name is called The Word of God. And the armies which were in heaven followed him upon white horses, clothed in fine linen, white and clean. And out of his mouth goeth a sharp sword, that with it he should smite the nations: and he shall rule them with a rod of iron: and he treadeth the winepress of the fierceness and wrath of Almighty God. And he hath on his vesture and on his thigh a name written, KING OF KINGS, AND LORD OF LORDS.

Thus, we receive a simple answer to our question, "Who is the woman?" The woman is the nation of Israel, which brought forth the Son, and the Son Himself testified, "Salvation is of the Jews."

It is significant that believers find their identity in this Ruler, as revealed in Revelation 2:26-27: "And he that overcometh, and keepeth my works unto the end, to him will I give power over the nations: And he shall rule them with a rod of iron; as the vessels of a potter shall they be broken to shivers: even as I received of my Father." Note that the phrase "he shall rule" refers to the believer. Jesus makes this promise to all who overcome. They will receive power "over the nations," and they (believers) shall "rule them with a rod of iron."

The Red Dragon

Parallel to the appearance of this woman is another significant event that is taking place. It is the "great red dragon." What does this dragon do? It casts "the third part of the stars of heaven...to the earth" (verse 4). Obviously, these are not literal stars. The earth is just one of innumerable planets in the universe. It is just a speck of dust when compared to some of the stars. A third of the stars of heaven have no room on planet Earth; therefore, we must return to heavenly realities. This is taking place "in heaven." We are dealing with spiritual realities.

Who Are the Fallen Stars?

Doubtless these fallen stars are fallen angels. Jude wrote about them in verse 6, "And the angels which kept not their first estate, but left their own habitation, he hath reserved in everlasting chains under darkness unto the judgment of the great day."

Let's read Daniel 8:10 as a cross-reference: "And it waxed great, even to the host of heaven; and it cast down some of the host and of the stars to the ground, and stamped upon them." Verse 11 reveals that this is the Antichrist: "Yea, he magnified himself even to the prince of the host, and by him the daily sacrifice was taken away, and the place of his sanctuary was cast down." Self-magnification is one of Satan's main characteristics. But note here that this identity is described in the previous verse as the "little horn" "cast down some of the host of the stars to the ground." Therefore, it is clear that this identity has power over the stars; that is, the fallen angels, and they become subject to Him. The Antichrist is the opposite of Christ, the human substitute for the real. Jesus did not magnify Himself, He debased Himself.

The Morning Star

We must also remember that Satan is identified as a star. Isaiah 14:12 describes his fall: "How art thou fallen from heaven, O Lucifer, son of the morning! how art thou cut down to the ground, which didst weaken the nations!" Martin Luther translated this verse as "O beautiful, star of the morning." And the

Tanakh states: "O shining one, son of dawn." I believe that "morning star" is the best translation, because it points to the imitation of "the bright and morning star." Here we must read the testimony of Jesus Himself: "I Jesus have sent mine angel to testify unto you these things in the churches. I am the root and the offspring of David, and the bright and morning star" (Revelation 22:16).

We may also add that the word "star" is used in reference to the Church in Revelation 1:20: "The mystery of the seven stars...The seven stars are the angels of the seven churches." And in Revelation 2:28, the promise is given to the overcomer: "And I will give him the morning star." Therefore, when the Bible speaks about stars, in this case, it makes reference to two categories: 1) the demonic stars and 2) Jesus, the Bright and Morning Star and His own.

The devil rules the demonic world. He possesses the power to "cast down some of the host and of the stars to the ground."

Revelation 12 describes a battle between God's intention to save mankind and Satan's intention to destroy God's creation.

Satan's Ultimate Mistake

The great dragon, identified as the old serpent called the devil and Satan, aimed "to devour her child as soon as it was born" (Revelation 12:4). But Satan failed to destroy the man-child.

We must remember that all of humanity is in darkness. It lies in sin, and is hopelessly lost for all of eternity. Satan knew about the child who would come and defeat him, but apparently he did not know the details. Who would have thought that Jesus, the Son of God and the Son of man, would defeat Satan by not fighting, but by voluntarily laying down His life in order to pave the way for mankind's salvation?

Surely Satan and the fallen angels must have rejoiced when Jesus hung helplessly on the cross and shouted "My God, my God, why hast thou forsaken me?" (Matthew 27:46). The inhabitants of hell must have broken out in laughter when they saw Jesus die on Calvary's cross. That was Satan's apparent victory.

However, he certainly was shocked when Jesus triumphantly arose on the third day and proclaimed victory over death, the devil and hell!

How did Jesus do it? By allowing the devil to take an innocent life. That was a first in human history. Jesus never sinned: He was perfect, He never gave into the temptations of the flesh, and He always did the will of His Father in heaven. With the death of this innocent man, Satan committed his ultimate mistake in that he caused evil man to crucify the Son of God, the only One who had never committed sin.

The door of salvation was now opened to all who would believe that Jesus died on Calvary's cross for their sins. From that point forward, people could take advantage of the payment Jesus paid for the penalty of sin.

Important to emphasize is that simple faith in the finished work causes the heavenly reaction that results in our rebirth. We must remember that man originally fell into sin by believing Satan's words rather than the Word of God. Now man can be reconciled to God by believing the words that Jesus Christ died for his sin.

Thus, we see the first five verses of Revelation 12 reveal the compact history of Israel, through whom God gave the Law, the prophets and the Son. Satan was a defeated enemy from that point forward. No longer could he openly appear and demand his rights to humanity, because now there was One who fully paid the sin debt of humanity, which means the devil lost his legal rights to any soul who comes to Jesus in faith seeking forgiveness.

Invisible Powers

"And there was war in heaven: Michael and his angels fought against the dragon; and the dragon fought and his angels, And prevailed not; neither was their place found any more in heaven. And the great dragon was cast out, that old serpent, called the Devil, and Satan, which deceiveth the whole world: he was cast out into the earth, and his angels were cast out with him" (Revelation 12:7-9).

Further analyzing Chapter 12, we find no names, political entities, or earthly definitions in relation to these great wonders taking place. But we do know that Michael and his angels will evict the great dragon from the heavenly places. The Bible simply states that the devil and his host "prevailed not, neither was their place found any more in heaven" (verse 8).

This is a heavenly wonder, a miracle of God's grace. You see God is not a dictator. He does not deal with the enemy unilaterally. After all, the devil does have a legal right to be in the presence of God, because man is sinful; subsequently, he who sins is a servant to sin and is subject to the devil. But this legal right is annulled by the fact that Jesus paid for the sins of the repentant person. As a result, the rug is pulled out from under the devil's feet.

The Accuser of the Brethren

Verse 10 contains a reference to what is happening on earth. When Satan is cast out of heaven, "the accuser of our brethren is cast down, which accused them before our God day and night" (verse 10). Thus, the Church can no longer be on earth. Satan and his host will be cast from heaven to earth the moment the Rapture takes place and we are drawn to heaven. This seems like a parallel event; the devil is cast out of heaven while believers are raptured *into* heaven.

Satan is hard at work accusing the brethren 24 hours a day. Why does he do that? Because of sin. Saints are pardoned sinners, nothing more; thus, they are the target of the "accuser." The devil tells God all who sin belong to him. He may point to the written Word and say, "Look, it is written, 'He who sins is of the devil.'"

That's where the miracle of grace begins: "Jesus paid it all, all to Him I owe, sin hath left a crimson stain, He washed it white as snow" ("Jesus Paid It All," written by Elvina M. Hall, 1865). We have an advocate, one who stands on our behalf and says, "I have paid the price for his or her sins."

Why is Satan cast out of heaven? The answer is simple: all the saints on earth will be translated into perfection when the Rapture takes place. Being perfect takes away Satan's right to accuse us before the throne of God. At that very moment, there is no spot or wrinkle in the Church; it is absolutely pure and perfect.

We read about the Rapture in 1 Corinthians 15:52-56:

> In a moment, in the twinkling of an eye, at the last trump: for the trumpet shall sound, and the dead shall be raised incorruptible, and we shall be changed. For this corruptible must put on incorruption, and this mortal must put on immortality. So when this corruptible shall have put on incorruption, and this mortal shall have put on immortality, then shall be brought to pass the saying that is written, Death is swallowed up in victory. O death, where is thy sting? O grave, where is thy victory? The sting of death is sin; and the strength of sin is the law.

We will be changed. Nothing sinful will remain in us. We will leave our sinful tabernacles of flesh and blood, and we will be translated into the glorious image of the Beloved. Now the devil has no one to accuse before God; subsequently, his job is done, he is cast out.

The Great Contrast

Next we see a vision that simultaneously shows the most horrendous situation on planet Earth and the most glorious time in heaven: "Therefore rejoice, ye heavens, and ye that dwell in them. Woe to the inhabitants of the earth and of the sea! for the devil is come down unto you, having great wrath, because he knoweth that he hath but a short time" (verse 12).

The saints are in heavenly places. But God's people (Israel) are in dire need, because Satan is now trying to destroy the nation of Israel: "And when the dragon saw that he was cast unto the earth, he persecuted the woman which brought forth the man child. And to the woman were given two wings of a great eagle, that she might fly into the wilderness, into her place, where she is nourished for a time, and times, and half a time, from the face of the serpent" (verses 13-14). The woman (Israel) is now miraculously being protected as she flies into the wilderness and is kept safe from the serpent.

Where is the Wilderness?

Here again we must be careful to not read something into the text that has not been written. We don't know if this is a wilderness meaning a desert, or a wilderness among the nations of the world. The only thing we know for sure is that she is protected.

Many scholars believe that the location of the wilderness is the red rock city in Jordan called Petra. But we can only arrive at that conclusion by using an extended interpretation. Besides, there is not enough room for all the Jews in that relatively small place. Nor is there enough water or food, and surely it is a dangerous place. Petra is surrounded by mountains. If all the Jews escaped to that place, only a few bombs or missiles would guarantee virtually total destruction. Because of the uncertainty of such interpretation, I think it's best to leave Scripture the way it is: "And the woman fled into the wilderness, where she hath a place prepared of God, that they should feed her there a thousand two hundred and threescore days" (Revelation 12:6). I believe that when God prepares a place, it will not be holes in the ground or caves in a mountain, but 10-star hotels with all the accommodations necessary to exist in a modern functioning civilization. So the bottom line is that God prepares a place for them, a place that is safe and secure for almost $3^{1/2}$ years.

We must also point out once again that this speaks from a heavenly perspective. The serpent persecuted the seed of the woman before Jesus was born. Long ago, when Israel became a nation in the land of Egypt, the serpent used Pharaoh to destroy God's people. Since then Israel has been hated, persecuted and whenever possible, killed. Some historians estimate that more than 14 million Jews have been murdered since the 70 A.D. destruction of the temple in Jerusalem. The most horrendous murder of all time took place in Germany under Hitler's rule when more than 6 million Jews were systematically killed and incinerated.

Revelation 12 provides an overview of the past, present and future heavenly powers in relationship to Satan's power. Chapter 13 reveals Satan's cunning devices, and how he takes hold of all who dwell upon the earth through his deceptive methods to implement final and total control of all people on earth with his created image and the Mark of the Beast.

Chapter 9

DEMONIC DOMINANCE OF THE UNDERWORLD

L et's take another look at the powers of darkness because they are the initiating forces that guide the people on planet Earth. Satan is the god of this world; he has successfully deceived all of humanity, with the exception of the true Church of Jesus Christ. His intentions are clear: he wants greater dominion over each person until he finally receives worship from all of mankind.

Mystery Babylon

And he had power to give life unto the image of the beast, that the image of the beast should both speak, and cause that as many as would not worship the image of the beast should be killed. And he causeth all, both small and great, rich and poor, free and bond, to receive a mark in their right hand, or in their foreheads: And that no man might buy or sell, save he that had the mark, or the name of the beast, or the number of his name... And I saw three unclean spirits like frogs come out of the mouth of the dragon, and out of the mouth of the beast, and out of the mouth of the false prophet. For they are the spirits of devils, working miracles, which go forth unto the kings of the earth and of the whole world, to gather them to the battle of that great day of God Almighty (Revelation 13:15-17; 16:13-14).

For all nations have drunk of the wine of the wrath of her fornication, and the kings of the earth have committed fornication with her, and the merchants of the earth are waxed rich through the abundance of her delicacies (Revelation 18:3).

These few verses describe what will happen in the future. But we must reemphasize that the preparation for the invisible demonic powers of the underworld to be physically manifested on planet Earth are in full progress. Let's not make the mistake and pass this on for some future time because preparations for the fulfillment have been in the works for almost 2,000 years, particularly since the birth of the Church of Jesus Christ at Pentecost in Jerusalem.

We have read about the glory and the fall of Mystery Babylon. It revealed that the entire world ("all nations") is involved: the kings of the earth are the political leaders, and the merchants of the earth represent the world's financial and economic system.

Notice that the passage speaks of Babylon, which is a historical city, but one defined as being global: "the great, the mother of harlots, abominations of the earth" (Revelation 17:5). This is part of the big end-time picture and refers to a time when the world will have united under one global religion and one global economy. Total control through the Mark of the Beast will have become a reality. No earthly power structure will be able to oppose the Antichrist because Revelation 13:4 states: "who is able to make war with him?" One leader will be in charge of world security for the first time in history; thus, we will have a truly global system on earth.

Literal or Spiritual?

We must answer one important question before we proceed: Are these events literal, or should they be interpreted spiritually? Here is the description of Babylon:

> So he carried me away in the spirit into the wilderness: and I saw a woman sit upon a scarlet coloured beast, full of names of blasphemy, having seven heads and ten horns. And the woman was arrayed in purple and scarlet colour, and decked with gold and precious stones and pearls, having a golden cup in her hand full of abominations and filthiness of her fornication: And upon her forehead was a name written, MYSTERY, BABYLON THE GREAT, THE MOTHER OF HARLOTS AND ABOMINATIONS OF THE EARTH (Revelation 17:3-5).

This is an extremely negative description, characterized by such words as: beast, blasphemy, abomination, filthiness, fornication. Please keep those words in mind, because they describe our world today. Note that they don't just speak of the so-called trash of our society — such as criminals, pornographers, drug addicts, sodomites, and prostitutes — but they paint an accurate portrait of the state of all segments of the world today. That is the glory of the world, the goal of all people on planet Earth. They strive for self-glory, wealth, security and power.

When we analyze Mystery Babylon, we need not imagine a literal woman riding upon some unknown animal that has seven heads and ten horns. To imagine such a scenario will only lead us into confusion. We must remember that John was being called into the future; he was seeing things from an eternal perspective. The angel "carried him away in the spirit." Spiritual things must be discerned spiritually, and not physically.

However, this spiritual vision is connected to the earth. Revelation 17:2 says: "With whom the kings of the earth have committed fornication, and the inhabitants of the earth have been made drunk with the wine of her fornication." Here we are clearly dealing with the political, economic and religious leaders of the world.

Revelation 17 provides a view of the earth from heaven. We have already listed the negative characteristics of this woman from a heavenly perspective, but seen from an earthly view, we read words such as "purple," "scarlet color," "gold," "precious stones" and "pearls." None of those items are evil in and of themselves. Actually, they are desirable. But what looks good on earth does not necessarily look good from heaven.

Therefore, we are simultaneously dealing with spiritual and earthly realities.

Who Is This Woman?

"And I saw the woman drunken with the blood of the saints, and with the blood of the martyrs of Jesus: and when I saw her, I wondered with great admiration" (verse 6). Again, we must realize that we are not speaking about a real woman who has literally drunk the blood of the saints of Jesus. Picturing the prophetic Word in such a manner is just as dangerous as when we imagine the devil with a pitchfork, a tail and two horns on his head. The Bible does not reveal such an identity.

The last verse of Chapter 17 answers the question, "Who is Mystery Babylon?" "And the woman which thou sawest is that great city, which reigneth over the kings of the earth." Now the "woman" is identified as the "great city."

Doubtless, we are confronted here with the demonic forces of the invisible world. But these forces become visibly manifested through a city and a system that becomes the most powerful in all of history: "which reigneth over the kings of the earth."

John was understandably puzzled: "I wondered with great admiration." The Twentieth Century New

Testament says: "I was amazed beyond measure." He never had seen anything quite like it. His surprise did not remain hidden, for we read: "And the angel said unto me, Wherefore didst thou marvel?" (Revelation 17:7). Then the angel offered a revelation: "I will tell thee the mystery of the woman, and of the beast that carrieth her, which hath the seven heads and ten horns. The beast that thou sawest was, and is not; and shall ascend out of the bottomless pit, and go into perdition: and they that dwell on the earth shall wonder, whose names were not written in the book of life from the foundation of the world, when they behold the beast that was, and is not, and yet is" (verses 7-8).

Who is this beast? Doubtless, it is Satan. He is the origin of sin, rebellion, death and destruction. However, this beast must take on bodily form to constitute a political identity, which will climax under the identity of the Antichrist.

Is Babylon Lucifer?

In order not to confuse spiritual matters with the earthly matters, let us read Isaiah 14, which documents Satan's origin. The subject is introduced with these words: "That thou shalt take up this proverb against the king of Babylon, and say, How hath the oppressor ceased! the golden city ceased!" (Isaiah 14:4). There is no need for interpretation; this verse speaks about the literal, physical king of Babylon. The passage continues: "How art thou fallen from

132

heaven, O Lucifer, son of the morning! how art thou cut down to the ground, which didst weaken the nations! For thou hast said in thine heart, I will ascend into heaven, I will exalt my throne above the stars of God: I will sit also upon the mount of the congregation, in the sides of the north: I will ascend above the heights of the clouds; I will be like the most High" (verses 12-14).

With these words we enter a different realm that cannot be identified with someone on earth, or with the king of Babylon. This is the story of the fall of the son of morning, popularly known in English as Lucifer. But the contact person through whom Lucifer is identified in this case is the king of Babylon. Yet clearly, Babylon is not Lucifer.

Is Lucifer the King of Tyrus?

Another example is found in Ezekiel 28. Here the words are directed against "the king of Tyrus." Again, no further explanation is needed: the king of Tyrus is the king of Tyrus. But a new identity is revealed when we read further:

Thus saith the Lord GOD; Because thine heart is lifted up, and thou hast said, I am a God, I sit in the seat of God, in the midst of the seas; yet thou art a man, and not God, though thou set thine heart as the heart of God: Behold, thou art wiser than Daniel; there is no secret that they can hide from thee: With thy wisdom and with thine under-standing thou hast gotten thee riches, and hast gotten gold and silver into thy treasures: By thy great wisdom and by thy traffick hast thou increased thy riches, and thine heart is lifted up because of thy riches: Therefore thus saith the Lord GOD; Because thou hast set thine heart as the heart of God; Behold, therefore I will bring strangers upon thee, the terrible of the nations: and they shall draw their swords against the beauty of thy wisdom, and they shall defile thy brightness. They shall bring thee down to the pit, and thou shalt die the deaths of them that are slain in the midst of the seas. Wilt thou yet say before him that slayeth thee, I am God? but thou shalt be a man, and no God, in the hand of him that slayeth thee. Thou shalt die the deaths of the uncircumcised by the hand of strangers: for I have spoken it, saith the Lord GOD (verses 1-10).

While this is still addressed to the king of Tyrus, we understand that with the statement, "hath set thine heart as the heart of God," the identity is no longer limited to the king of Tyrus. Here we begin to see the revelation of a demonic force behind the king.

Further reading makes it clear that this speaks of Lucifer:

Moreover the word of the LORD came unto me, saying, Son of man, take up a lamentation upon the king of Tyrus, and say unto him, Thus saith the Lord GOD; Thou sealest up the sum, full of wisdom, and perfect in beauty. Thou hast been in Eden the garden of God; every precious

> stone was thy covering, the sardius, topaz, and the diamond, the beryl, the onyx, and the jasper, the sapphire, the emerald, and the carbuncle, and gold: the workmanship of thy tabrets and of thy pipes was prepared in thee in the day that thou wast created. Thou art the anointed cherub that covereth; and I have set thee so: thou wast upon the holy mountain of God; thou hast walked up and down in the midst of the stones of fire. Thou wast perfect in thy ways from the day that thou wast created, till iniquity was found in thee (verses 11-15).

No doubt this is speaking about the father of lies, who was a murderer from the beginning. How do we know? Because the king of Tyrus was never "perfect in beauty." He never had "precious stone as his covering." Never was the king of Tyrus "the anointed cherub" and never had he "walked up and down in the midst of the stones of fire." And he most definitely never was "perfect in his ways." This is a reverse prophecy about the fall of the "son of the morning," who became Satan.

Therefore, the beast with the seven heads and ten horns does not need to be identified with a geographical country or a physical personality. In other words, Mystery Babylon is not the literal city of Babylon located in the territory of today's Iraq. (I must add, neither is it the city of Rome exclusively; it is Rome globally.)

Topographical Identity

"And here is the mind which hath wisdom. The seven heads are seven mountains, on which the woman sitteth" (Revelation 17:9). Seven mountains identify the topography of where the contact between the demonic forces and an earthly leadership will be established.

Mystery Babylon is a city, one built on seven mountains. We don't have to search far and wide to find the most famous city in the world that is built on seven mountains: Rome. Literal Babylon is built on the Euphrates River. The land is flat with no mountains.

Above and beyond these facts, we must turn to the Scripture, which clearly tells us that Rome is the last empire. There is no evidence that Babylon, the first empire, will be resurrected to play a key role in the endtimes.

Demonic Powers

Now we come to verses 10-12: "And there are seven kings: five are fallen, and one is, and the other is not yet come; and when he cometh, he must continue a short space. And the beast that was, and is not, even he is the eighth, and is of the seven, and goeth into perdition. And the ten horns which thou sawest are ten kings, which have received no kingdom as yet; but receive power as kings one hour with the beast." Should we assume these are literal, physical kings with a political identity, or are we dealing with ten kings who rule ten demonic power structures?

I am a literal interpreter of Scripture, but when I see no further identification, such as names, places and dates, then I fail to see the evidence that would lead me to conclude that there will be ten earthly kings with ten earthly kingdoms.

Demonic Dominion

Again, let us return to Isaiah 14, which speaks about the fall of the "son of the morning." As already mentioned, this prophecy is addressed to the king of Babylon. Then we are given a vision of hell with an important lesson: "Hell from beneath is moved for thee to meet thee at thy coming: it stirreth up the dead for thee, even all the chief ones of the earth; it hath raised up from their thrones all the kings of the nations" (Isaiah 14:9). Clearly this is not speaking about the literal leaders of the world, but of demonic powers, the chief (leaders) of the earth, "the kings of the nations." This identifies the invisible power structure of hell, which stands behind the visible political power structure.

For clearer insight, let's read the Tenakh in English: "Sheol below was astir to greet your coming — Rousing, for you the shades of all earth's chieftains, raising from their thrones all the kings of nations. All speak up and say to you, So you have been stricken as we were, you have become like us! Your pomp is brought down to Sheol, and the strains of your lutes! Worms are to be your bed, maggots your blanket!" (verses 9-11).

The German Menge translation states, "The kingdom of the death below is stirred up for your sake in the expectation of your arrival: the shadows are disturbed because of you and all who have gone before you, the heads of the leaders of the earth and all the kings of the nations are caused to arise from the bondage of their thrones, they all lift up their voices and call unto you: thou hast become sick unto death. You have become like one of us, you have been made equal unto us! Cast down into the kingdom of the death is all your glory, the sound of your harps! Maggots make up your bed beneath you and worms form your blanket!"

From these verses we learn there is a demonic power structure in "hell...beneath" and the "kings of the nations" are Satan's underlings — the demonic rulers and chief of the earth. This entire scenario is taking place in the invisible world, in the kingdom of the dead in hell. This does not speak about live people, much less live kings. This is the demonic dominion of the underworld.

Ten Horns — Ten Kings?

Revelation 17:12 says, "And the ten horns which thou sawest are ten kings, which have received no kingdom as yet; but receive power as kings one hour with the beast." Here is an additional reason to place these ten kings into Satan's demonic power structure, because they receive power "as kings one hour." No politician can do anything in an hour, other than perhaps drink a cup of coffee. But this becomes quite a different story in the spiritual world.

Lucifer will still possess certain powers even though he will be exposed as a loser. These "ten kings" will surrender their power in support of Lucifer. Ten demonic powers will be in charge of planet Earth. This relates to the Scriptures revealing that the prince of darkness rules this world.

What do they do? "These have one mind, and shall give their power and strength unto the beast" (verse 13). We should not expect ten kings who receive ten physical, geographically identifiable kingdoms, because no political leader, including a king, has the means to hand over power to the beast: Satan himself. This is referring to the spiritual world.

Have you seen the devil lately? Of course not! Therefore, we must conclude that these are ten demonic kings who are in charge of the earth, and are in a league with the beast and the Antichrist, who is the visible manifestation of Satan.

Besides, we no longer have kings, and those who still carry that title are virtually insignificant. They do not possess the same unique power as a king. When we take the word "king" literally, then the meaning is demonic kings, since they do not fit the definition of an earthly king.

Prince of Persia

Another example is recorded in Daniel 10. After Daniel prayed for 21 days, we read:

> And he said unto me, O Daniel, a man greatly
> beloved, understand the words that I speak unto
> thee, and stand upright: for unto thee am I now
> sent. And when he had spoken this word unto me,
> I stood trembling. Then said he unto me, Fear not,
> Daniel: for from the first day that thou didst set
> thine heart to understand, and to chasten thyself
> before thy God, thy words were heard, and I am
> come for thy words. But the prince of the kingdom
> of Persia withstood me one and twenty days: but,
> lo, Michael, one of the chief princes, came to help
> me; and I remained there with the kings of Persia
> (Daniel 10:11-13).

The words are clear: "the prince of the kingdom of Persia." Who is this prince of Persia? It's definitely not a human being, because a human cannot oppose a messenger of God. Besides, Daniel was greatly loved and respected by the king of Babylon and later by the king of Persia. In fact, he was envied by his colleagues because of the excellent relationship he had with the royal house. Therefore, when we read in verse 13, "the prince of the kingdom of Persia withstood me," we know that it does not refer to an earthly human being but to an entity in the invisible world.

For a better understanding, I must quote Ephesians 6:12 again: "For we wrestle not against flesh and blood, but against principalities, against powers, against the rulers of the darkness of this world, against spiritual wickedness in high places." Daniel did not wrestle against flesh and blood, but against the spiritual powers under the heavens ruled by the king of darkness.

Errors in Interpretation

During the last few decades, we have made many mistakes in our attempt to identify physical entities by placing them in specific geographic regions, which leads to a misunderstanding of the prophetic Word.

Many of us remember that the European Common Market began in 1951 with six founding nations: Belgium, Germany, Luxemburg, France, Italy and Netherlands. Applications from Denmark, Ireland, Norway and the UK were being negotiated in 1970. At that time, many Bible prophecy scholars regarded the identity of the nations they thought represented the ten kings of the endtimes. The theory that those nations represented the ten kings became common knowledge when Denmark, Ireland and Britain were accepted into the Union in 1973.

Midnight Call Ministries founder, Dr. Wim Malgo, responded to such theories in 1967: "Let us not look for ten countries being members of the European Common Market constituting the fulfillment of Revelation 17:12. Rather, we must look for ten power structures that will develop through the European initiative, but will be worldwide."

The Visible and Invisible Kingdom

Before we go any further, let's summarize: God is the Creator of heaven and earth. Satan rebelled, and with him one-third of the angelic host left their habitation. That, however, did not negate God's plan of creation, salvation and restitution. He chose one man, Abraham, called the father of all believers, and used him to build a nation called Israel. The nation of Israel gave birth to the Savior. God's goal was to establish His kingdom on earth, which is evident from the message Jesus preached when He began His ministry: "Repent: for the kingdom of heaven is at hand" (Matthew 4:17). He continued preaching the same message heralded by John the Baptist: "Repent ye: for the kingdom of heaven is at hand" (Matthew 3:2). Later, Jesus commanded His disciples to do likewise, but He emphasized that this message was for Israel: "Go not into the way of the Gentiles, and into any city of the Samaritans enter ye not. But go rather to the lost sheep of the house of Israel. And as ye go, preach, saying, The kingdom of heaven is at hand" (Matthew 10:5-7).

These and other statements clearly reinforce the fact that God intends to establish His kingdom on earth, and therefore it is no surprise that the devil tries to do likewise. He, too, will establish his kingdom of his peace on earth, but it will be a peace that is based on lies and deception.

The New Nation

Israel rejected the kingdom by rejecting the King; thus, we read in Matthew 21:43: "Therefore say I unto you, The kingdom of God shall be taken from you, and given to a nation bringing forth the fruits thereof."

What is this nation that "bringeth forth the fruits?" It is the new nation, the Church of Jesus Christ. It is the invisible kingdom of believers, those who are saved through faith in Jesus Christ. Instead of believing the father of lies, we believe the truth. We follow Abraham, the father of all believers in the Word of God.

Believers from all over the world are being added to the Church daily and will continue to be added until the last Gentile person has been saved. The Church presents truth on planet Earth; we are a source of light to a dark world. This Church is unique. It is not limited to a country, language or culture, but is truly global. Members of this Church are pilgrims on this earth who have but one desire: to prepare for the coming of the Lord Jesus. The Church continues to be built, and Romans 11:25 will be fulfilled when the last of the Gentiles has been added. At that point, the complete and perfected invisible kingdom will be transferred into the presence of the Lord via the Rapture.

The Imitator

This should assist us in our understanding of what is taking place in the invisible world. God has promised to establish His visible kingdom in Israel, and from there rule the entire world in righteousness and justice. The devil's goal is to present his kingdom

143

to the world. He, too, is proclaiming through his servants, "Repent, for the kingdom of heaven is at hand," but his is a fake kingdom that will not produce the desired peace because sin will not have been appropriately dealt with.

Remember, the devil already is the legitimate ruler, or "god," of this world. The Bible says that those who sin are of the devil, and since all have sinned, then all are of the devil (1 John 3:8). Thus, we understand that Satan has one specific enemy: the Church of Jesus Christ. For that reason, he has infiltrated the Church in order to replace the message with his own convoluted message of health, wealth and prosperity for all people here and now. That message is contrary to Scripture, but most don't realize it.

Let us again read 2 Corinthians 11:4;13-15:

> For if he that cometh preacheth another Jesus, whom we have not preached, or if ye receive another spirit, which ye have not received, or another gospel, which ye have not accepted, ye might well bear with him.... For such are false apostles, deceitful workers, transforming themselves into the apostles of Christ. And no marvel; for Satan himself is transformed into an angel of light. Therefore it is no great thing if his ministers also be transformed as the ministers of righteousness; whose end shall be according to their works.

It stands to reason that he is eager to destroy the Church in opposition to Jesus' statement to build His

Church. "And the gates of hell shall not prevail against it" (Matthew 16:18).

Unfortunately, Churchianity's proclamation of a false Jesus is extremely popular. Nevertheless, true believers will follow the voice of the Good Shepherd, regardless of their circumstances or the risk of persecution.

We must add here that Satan's authority is limited to the permission granted him by God the Creator. If he could do as he pleased, then he most certainly would have successfully destroyed Israel and the Church by now.

Israel: The Hindering Element

God is also bound by His own promise to Abraham of a physical kingdom clearly defined by geographic borders extending from the Euphrates River to the river of Egypt.

Darkness will cover the earth after the Church has been raptured. Satan will be able to seduce people during this short period by using lying signs and wonders so that humanity will worship the dragon. Although the devil already is the god of this world, he lacks one thing: worship. He desires to receive the worship that belongs only to God. Therefore, the devil must continue to execute his deceptive plan until "all that dwell upon the earth shall worship him" (Revelation 13:8).

Once he reaches that point, Satan will recognize that there is still one problem: the Jews. Therefore, he will persecute them to the utmost. At that time, God will supernaturally intervene and Jesus will return for Israel. The Bible says that His feet will stand upon the Mount of Olives, and at that point, Israel will experience salvation while the rest of the world will come under God's destructive judgment.

War Against the Lamb

Back to the ten kings. "And the ten horns which thou sawest are ten kings, which have received no kingdom as yet; but receive power as kings one hour with the beast" (Revelation 17:12). The kings will give their power and authority to the beast. Verse 14 explains why: "These shall make war with the Lamb, and the Lamb shall overcome them: for he is Lord of lords, and King of kings: and they that are with him are called, and chosen, and faithful." Here again we learn that these are not literal, earthly kings, but they are powers of darkness. No matter how diabolic and sinful man is he cannot wage war against the Lamb. The Lamb is unreachable, untouchable and invisible to humans. You can't fight something that is invisible.

Please keep this fact in mind; it will help you to understand the development toward the Mark of the Beast.

Problem in the Demonic Ranks

"And the ten horns which thou sawest upon the beast, these shall hate the whore, and shall make her desolate and naked, and shall eat her flesh, and burn

146

her with fire" (verse 16). Satan, who is manifested through the appearance of the Antichrist, represents the power structure of the visible world. It consists of the devil and his angelic hosts, coupled with the ten demonic kings. They work in conjunction with the earthly, visible power structure identified as "Mystery Babylon the great, the mother of harlots and abomination of the earth," which represents the global religious world, including Churchianity.

The whore is the one who "reigneth over the kings of the earth." That is a key to the conflict. The whore has both political and religious power. Note that God gives a kingdom to the beast: "For God hath put in their hearts to fulfil his will, and to agree, and give their kingdom unto the beast, until the words of God shall be fulfilled" (Revelation 17:17).

Religion Rules

In the last few decades, we've seen the development of a religious, political philosophy, particularly manifested in the Muslim world. In other words, religions rule! A similar thing happened in the Hindu world when India's prime minister attempted to turn that nation into a Hindu republic. He has since lost his office, but the example shows that the tendency to mix politics with religion is very popular.

It is clear that religion in the United States plays a major role in political developments. Even Bible-believing Christians have jumped on the Neo-Dominion theology bandwagon. What is

Neo-Dominion theology? In brief, it is a belief that we have received a mandate to change the world, particularly our country. Neo-Dominionists propose that peace, justice and righteousness will be established by the formation of a Christian government. Many well-meaning Christians believe that if the government is saturated with Christians, then laws favorable to Christians will be passed. Obviously, they overlook the fact that any law relating to religion, regardless of its type, will be taken advantage of by others. They forget that the Church cannot be legislated by political powers. That has been tried by the Roman Catholic Church, which exercised supreme political power during most of its history. If Christianity takes over the functioning government, then essentially it becomes anti-Christianity.

God and the European Union

Europe already travels in a direction contrary to the rest of the world. People from a number of nations are offended because unlike most other countries, God has been omitted from the Constitution. This seems prophetic, because the political entity described in verses 10-13 that have subjected themselves to the religious authority will ultimately destroy the religious power structure: "And the ten horns which thou sawest upon the beast, these shall hate the whore, and shall make her desolate and naked, and shall eat her flesh, and burn her with fire" (Revelation 17:16).

In light of this fact, let's read an article about the pope's book that appeared in the *Jerusalem Post*:

> Pope Benedict XVI rails against Europe in his first book published since becoming pope, chastising a culture that he says excludes God from life and allows innocent lives — the unborn — to be taken from God through legalized abortion.
>
> Ratzinger takes as a starting point the decision of European Union leaders to exclude a reference to Europe's Christian roots from the preamble of the proposed EU constitution, whose future remains uncertain following its rejection by French and Dutch voters in recent referendums.
>
> The Vatican had campaigned to have the reference included, part of its attempts to stem what it sees as a continent of increasingly empty churches that is often hostile to religion.
>
> "Europe has developed a culture which, in a way never before known to humanity, excludes God from public conscience, either by being denied or by judging his existence to be uncertain and thus belonging to subjective choices, something irrelevant for public life," Benedict writes.
>
> "It's not the mention of God that offends the followers of other religions, but precisely the attempt to build a human community absolutely without God," he writes.
>
> (*Jerusalem Post*, 22 June 2005, pg. 7).

This clearly reveals the strong desire for religion to

remain a part of the political process.

The difficulty, however, is identifying this "god." Is it the "god" of Churchianity, the Jews, the Muslims or the Hindus? Those are some of the reasons the framers of the European Union Constitution have deleted any reference to "god."

One thing is clear: Religion is a vital component of any civilized society, wherefore, even without any reference to "god" in the proposed constitution, Churchianity will remain an issue that will need to be dealt with. Religion in general and the Vatican in particular will play a major role in the future.

Also, it stands to reason that due to the pluralistic European society, the potential of accepting a substitute agreeable to all major religions becomes very realistic. We are reminded of 2 Thessalonians 2:11: "And for this cause God shall send them strong delusion, that they should believe a lie."

Chapter 10

THE SUBSTITUTE CHURCH

A political, religious institution will be necessary in order for the powers of darkness to use man in the Antichrist establishment of a visible and physical kingdom on earth. Therefore, instead of the Church of Jesus Christ, which is His Body, another church must be established and have many similarities so that it looks like the real thing.

The Imposter

Satan has devised a cunning plan in order to camouflage salvation in Jesus Christ by presenting himself as mankind's ultimate savior. An imposter is blocking the door to salvation, the only way of escape from eternal damnation. The devil's substitute salvation fits the desire of man's heart. How can we be protected from such deception? The answer is found in 1 Thessalonians 5:23: "And the very God of peace sanctify you wholly; and I pray God your whole spirit and soul and body be preserved blameless unto the coming of our Lord Jesus Christ." Born-again Christians follow the Lord wholeheartedly and they produce fruit of the Spirit: "But the fruit of the Spirit is love, joy, peace, longsuffering, gentleness, goodness, faith, meekness, temperance: against such there is no law" (Galatians 5:22-23). That is the protection against the Mark of the Beast.

All other people will welcome the great deception, the false Jesus, and the imitation gospel as proclaimed by the spirit of the Antichrist.

Unity at Any Cost

Earlier we read that the nations, the heads of state and the global economic power structure have committed fornication with Mystery Babylon. What does this mean? Obviously, it is a religious activity. Man wants to unite religion, politics and economy in order to produce unity, a one-world political system, a global, economic system and a world religious system.

We don't have to search far to realize that the ancient Greek-Roman system of democracy leads the world. Virtually all nations agree that democracy is the answer to the world's political conflicts.

We know the global economic system is so integrated that national borders no longer exist.

Religion is the biggest problem. There are four major religious groups: Christianity, Islam, Hinduism and Buddhism. Islam is the apparent danger to Western Christianity. Hinduism and Buddhism have entered into the Western World through various practices such as yoga, acupuncture, karate, judo, etc., and are accepted in general terms.

Regardless of the seemingly irreconcilable differences between religions, particularly between Christianity and Islam, the Bible makes it clear that all who live upon the earth will worship the image of the beast, the Antichrist.

The Power of Rome

The pope leads the largest Christian denomination and for the most part, he represents all of Christianity. Therefore, Rome is the most influential city in the world. Other cities such as London, Beijing and New York may be much more influential. But that is only the case when we observe this superficially. We must not forget that the Bible speaks of the long term: Rome existed when Jesus was born; today, it is serving as the headquarters of the largest religion in the world. It would be a mistake to replace Rome with some other city just because it exhibited some similarities to Bible prophecy.

Long-Term Prophecy

Daniel Chapter 2 makes it clear that there are only four Gentile superpowers: Babylon, Medo-Persia, Greece and Rome. Daniel 2:44 reveals important information: "And in the days of these kings shall the God of heaven set up a kingdom, which shall never be destroyed: and the kingdom shall not be left to other people, but it shall break in pieces and consume all these kingdoms, and it shall stand for ever." Note the time span: "in the days of these kings." That's more than 2,600 years. At this point, God has not established an earthly kingdom as prophesied; therefore, we know Rome is still an active player. Actually, it is playing the lead role on the global scale and will continue to do so until the day of final judgment when all Gentile authority is crushed. Therefore, the statement, "Rome ruled when Jesus was born and Rome will dominate when Jesus returns," is biblically correct.

Five Roman Continents

Also note that Europe, America, Australia, Africa, and most of Asia have been built on the foundation of Roman laws. The Europeans dominated the world through colonialism, thus putting their permanent mark on all five continents. North and South America are products of European colonization, and so is Australia. Virtually all of Africa and most of Asia was at one time subject to Europe. This corresponds to the prophetic Word, which identifies Rome as the last Gentile superpower.

The nations cannot properly communicate unless they use European principles, languages and methods. The entire global economy is built upon Roman political and business laws. The assumption that Rome has no global influence is a shortsighted analysis.

The Death of a Pope

This is a sensitive subject and many readers may take offense to this interpretation of prophecy, but the Bible says that we should not be ignorant of the devil's plans, therefore we must soberly analyze what Scripture teaches and what is being taught by the Roman Catholic Church hierarchy in particular, which, as we will see, does offer a substitute salvation.

A picture of Rome's world dominion was demonstrated at the funeral of Pope John Paul.

Born Karol Wojtyla in 1920 in Poland, Pope John Paul II would later be elected as Bishop of Rome on October 16, 1978.

Pope John was the leader of the world's largest religion, the most influential of moral teachers, the greatest political advisor and the most persistent proclaimer of peace for the entire world.

The Catholic News Service highlighted some of the many achievements of the popular Pope John Paul II:

> The April 8 funeral of Pope John Paul II may have marked his last diplomatic coup when more than 200 heads of state and government delegates — some bitter adversaries — came together to pay their last respects.
>
> U.S. President George W. Bush was just yards away from President Mohammed Khatami of Iran, a country he has labeled part of an 'axis of evil.' Khatami, who met with the pope in 1999, said the April 8 gathering should be a springboard for peace.

The article continued:

> 'The presence of such high-level world figures demonstrates the world's respect for the pope,' Khatami said: 'I wish this day could be a moment that makes us hope for a future of peace, not of conflict and hostility.'
>
> Representatives of troubled neighbors — India and Pakistan as well as Israel and the Palestinian National Authority — were seated in the same section reserved for heads of state in St. Peter's Square.
>
> Israeli President Moshe Katsav and Palestinian Prime Minister Ahmed Qureia were among the political leaders there who had met with the pope and, at times, had been praised and reproved by him.
>
> The Pope repeatedly voiced to Bush his strong disapproval over the invasion of Iraq, most recently during the president's June 2004 visit to the Vatican.
>
> But John Paul's funeral gave the world's leaders the opportunity for a fresh start. A senior Vatican official told reporters that the funeral gave these leaders a sense of freedom. They were not afraid that people would read their actions politically.
>
> 'I saw Israelis, Muslims who greeted each other with gestures of affection,' he said.

Other headlines included:

- "Pope John Paul II: Model of Heroic Faith"
- "In St. Peter's Square, a universal church says goodbye to Pope"
- "Latin America mourns death of 'a father' Pope John Paul II"

- "Israeli Prime Minister calls Pope a 'friend of the Jews'"
- "World Leaders voice sorrow, condolence over Pope's death"

Doubtless, Pope John Paul II was a courageous man who faithfully executed his office as the leader of the Catholic Church and stood alongside the masses of the poor and downtrodden, those who had little or no chance of making it in modern society. He pleaded for peace with all the politicians of the world.

The Power of Unity

Pope John Paul's funeral was the greatest gathering of world leaders of all time, demonstrating an amazing unifying spirit present in the whole world.

Why did all of these politicians and dignitaries come to the funeral? The attendance at Pope John Paul's funeral by the world leaders confirmed their confidence that unity is the answer to the world's problems. These politicians were morally obligated to attend the Pope's funeral to demonstrate their support for world unity, peace and prosperity for all people.

Attendance at the pope's funeral was not required by any law, yet virtually everyone felt obligated to participate. Why did the world leaders travel to Rome? Were they there by coincidence? Did they want to perform an expression of good will? That wouldn't make sense, since the Vatican is supposed to be a religious organization. We are reminded here of

Revelation 18:3: "For all nations have drunk of the wine of the wrath of her fornication, and the kings of the earth have committed fornication with her, and the merchants of the earth are waxed rich through the abundance of her delicacies."

We must also add that most of those heads-of-states had previously been granted an audience with the leader of the Catholic Church. An audience with the pope is a privilege. This is not a meeting of political equals; an audience provides an opportunity to have one's ideas heard. The president of the United States can request an audience with the pope, but the pope does not need to request an audience with the president.

So why did U.S. President George W. Bush, leader of an overwhelmingly Protestant country, attend Pope John Paul's funeral? Why did he and his predecessor have so many meetings with him? Granted, there are many possible answers to these questions, but we would probably all agree that none of our answers would be satisfactory to all. But one answer definitely fits: peace and security.

These Have One Mind

To better understand this event, we need to realize that this is the result of spiritual matters, things not visible to the world. John the Revelator saw ten horns and ten kings that we identified as demonic power, and revealed that they have one mind (Revelation 17:13). We cannot deny that all the world's leaders had "one mind": they were paying their respect and honor to one pope!

I must qualify this statement. These political leaders are not themselves evil spirits, nor do they wish to intentionally make war with the Lamb, which is the scripturally declared goal of these ten demon kings. But the world's political leaders honored a religion, and that religion, as we will see, is contrary to Scripture.

Amazing Similarities

Important to Bible believers is what Scripture reveals about the endtimes. One system will dominate the world and one leader in particular will become the benevolent führer of planet Earth. We call this man the Antichrist.

We have already asked how it will be possible for all who live on earth to worship the image of the beast. In order to identify the imposter church, we need to look for a system or person with the power to summon the leaders of the world for the benefit of mankind.

The statement, "I saw Israelis [and] Muslims who greeted each other with gestures of affection," has not been heard in modern times. Here we are confronted with a fact no one can deny; namely, that one man will be capable, even after his death, of uniting enemies in unprecedented ways.

I don't believe we are stretching our interpretation when we say that "the kings of the earth" went to

Rome to honor the power of peace, security and good will demonstrated by the man who had died.

Another paragraph of the *Catholic News Service* article states:

> Vatican Radio called the fathering of heads of state representing some 141 nations around the world 'a sort of planetary parliament, assembled for a special session under the sign of common prayer and human solidarity toward a pope who was loved by many near and far.'

Scripture or Man-Made Doctrine?

The staunch proclamation of human values, justice and liberty is one of the great hallmarks of the Catholic Church. Hundreds of thousands, if not millions are faithfully in the service of the Church. The Roman Catholic Church is the only organization in the world that is truly international. As a human organization, we must conclude that the Catholic Church is a good and benevolent organization. But are the doctrines of the Catholic Church scriptural or manmade? The catechism of the Catholic Church states this regarding the Bible:

> The inspired books teach the truth. Since therefore all that the inspired authors or sacred writers affirm should be regarded as affirmed by the Holy Spirit, we must acknowledge that the books of Scripture firmly, faithfully, and without error teach that truth which God, for the sake of our salvation, wished to see confided to the Sacred Scriptures (pg. 37, #107).

This is a clear affirmation of the truth of the Bible as set forth in the catechism and recognizes the inspiration of the Holy Scriptures.

However, article 2 of the same catechism states:

> It is clear therefore that, in the supremely wise arrangement of God, sacred Tradition, Sacred Scripture, and the Magisterium of the Church are so connected and associated that one of them cannot stand without the others. Working together, each in its own way, under the action of the one Holy Spirit, they all contribute effectively to the salvation of souls (pg. 34, #95).

This statement presents a great dilemma: Does the Bible need additional support in order for it to be authenticated? Does the Catholic Church confirm and accept that the Bible is God's full and final counsel to His Church? If so, how is it possible that the Word of God needs help from "sacred tradition" and "the mysteries of the church?"

The key conflict lies in the fact that the Catholic hierarchy claims to be the exclusive owner and dispenser of God's Word, making it the sole distributor of salvation.

We deliberately and emphatically want to distance ourselves from Catholic bashers. The Catholic Church is a benevolent organization, full of compassion and servitude. Although rarely reported in the United States media, it is quite common in Europe to see representatives of the Catholic Church be first in line to help after a natural disaster or catastrophe.

This organization is supported by hundreds of thousands of very dedicated men and women who have sworn to serve their church under the leadership of their pope.

In my personal business dealings, I have found Catholic men and women to be upright, respectful, honest and staunch supporters of family values. Who else is more capable of being on the spot to help others than the Catholic Church, with its missionaries placed in virtually every country in the world? As a matter of fact, the Vatican operates more international embassies than does the United States of America.

However, the Catholic Church's claim to be the sole mediator between God and man stands in blatant opposition to Holy Scripture, and that is where we must draw the line.

Scripture Alone

Born-again, Bible-believing Christians have only one authority. It is not dictated, dominated or enforced by a group of men, but by the Holy Spirit, who enlightened and enables us to distinguish between truth and falsehood, salvation and damnation. It is the written Word of God.

As Christians, we have direct access to God's throne of grace through Jesus Christ: "For there is one God, and one mediator between God and men, the man Christ Jesus" (1 Timothy 2:5). We categorically reject, therefore, any avenue of mediation other than Jesus Christ, the Son of the Living God.

Mother of God Church

However, the Catholic Church adds: "But while in the most Blessed Virgin the Church has already reached that perfection whereby she exists without spot or wrinkle, the faithful still strive to conquer sin and increase in holiness. And so they turn their eyes to Mary, in her, the Church is already the 'all-holy'" (pg. 239, #829).

This catechism was authorized by Pope John Paul, who wrote the following words in the Introduction:

> At the conclusion of this document presenting the Catechism of the Catholic Church, I beseech the Blessed Virgin Mary, Mother of the Incarnate Word and Mother of the Church, to support with her powerful intercession the catechetical work of the entire Church on every level, at this time when she is called to a new effort of evangelization. May the light of the true faith free humanity from the ignorance and slavery of sin in order to lead it to the only freedom worthy of the name (cf. Jn 8:32): that of life in Jesus Christ under the guidance of the Holy Spirit, here below and in the Kingdom of heaven, in the fullness of the blessed vision of God face to face (cf. 1 Corinthians 13:12; 2 Corinthians 5:6-8) (pg. 6).

The title, "Mother of the Church" makes it clear that an imposter is being presented through the catechism of the Catholic Church.

This statement opens another door for an additional mediator, which means another gospel is being preached that reveals another Jesus through another spirit.

An Open Door to a Global Religion

The key to the Vatican's success is to confirm the truth of Holy Scripture, on the one hand, but on the other hand, it opens the door to accommodate other religions.

Regarding Islam, the catechism states:

> The Church's relationship with the Muslims. The plan of salvation also includes those who acknowledge the Creator, in the first place amongst whom are the Muslims; these profess to hold the faith of Abraham, and together with us they adore the one, merciful God, mankind's judge on the last day (pg. 242, #841).

Furthermore, under the heading "The Church's Bond With Non-Christian Religion," we read:

> All nations form but one community. This is so because all stem from the one stock which God created to people the entire earth, and also because all share a common destiny, namely God. His providence, evident goodness, and saving designs extend to all against the day when the elect are gathered together in the holy city (pg. 243, #842).

The goal becomes clear: Unite all religions under one umbrella headed by the so-called Vicar of Christ. That is why "the Catholic Church recognizes in other religions that search among shadows and images for the God who is unknown, yet near, since He gives life and breath to all things and wants all man to be saved." Therefore, "To reunite all his children, scattered and led astray by sin, the Father willed to call the whole of humanity together into his Son's Church. The Church is the place where humanity must rediscover its unity and salvation. The Church is 'the world reconciled'" (pg. 243, #845).

Need we say more? The aim is clearly revealed: All people from all religions should become one; thus, all people of all religions will gladly receive the Mark of the Beast and will, according to Revelation 13:8, worship his image.

The Quest for Global Unity

We all agree that today, for the first time in modern history, we can see a development towards a one-world religion in conjunction with a one-world economy and a one-world political system: Roman democracy.

There is not one head of state that does not desire reconciliation with other nations. All should live with one another peacefully and all citizens should prosper. Religion, particularly Catholicism, becomes a significant avenue to accomplish this goal. No one in his right mind would oppose the reconciliation of the world, peace among the nations and prosperity for all people. And no one other than the pope could better verbalize, and then demonstrate it to the world. Subsequently, the "one-mind" requirement is in the process of fulfillment.

Papacy and Politics

Catholics are not surprised by the pope's power. Until recently, the pope enjoyed preeminent political clout that reached far beyond the ranks of Catholics. History clearly documents that the political power structure in Europe, the continent that dominated the world, was either influenced or dictated by the office of the pope. The Church was to be the head of the state; as a matter of fact, in the United Kingdom, the Queen of England is the head of the church. Today, religion is not ruling directly but it certainly exercises power and influence.

With this in mind, are we receiving a clearer picture as to the possible fulfillment of Revelation 18:3? Political leaders have recognized, especially since the fall of the Soviet Union, that no nation can properly function in a civilized manner without religion.

The New Global World

The political leaders of the world, however, do not stand on their own merits as politicians because they are too dependent upon their respective economies and financial systems. But that is the point of conflict. The Bible does not provide for unity between faith in the living God and government. Yet the enemy successfully manipulates people's minds so they can have the peace, security and prosperity they dream about and simultaneously have a leader that they can love, trust, hear and see.

166

In other words, a visible manifestation of a person who possesses political charisma and religious conviction is the candidate for Antichrist.

Gathering at Jerusalem

It is significant that at this gathering of the world's leaders at the Vatican to pay respect to the late pope, all were united against one: Israel. How do we know that? Because not one leader of any nation agrees with the biblical borders of the Promised Land. For example, the United States insists that the Golan, Judea and Samaria should be given to Arab settlers and that part of Jerusalem must become the capital of the Palestinian state. Interestingly, no one made such a proposal when Jordan occupied Jerusalem for 19 years until June 7, 1967.

The prophet Joel wrote about another gathering of nations 800 years before Christ was born: "I will also gather all nations, and will bring them down into the valley of Jehoshaphat, and will plead with them there for my people and for my heritage Israel, whom they have scattered among the nations, and parted my land" (Joel 3:2). United States President George W. Bush has publicly declared to the nation and to the world that a Palestinian state (in the midst of Israel) must be established. We must not forget that the U.S. is considered Israel's best friend, therefore we don't need to quote what lesser friends or enemies of Israel have said about the land of Israel.

Is the Pope the Antichrist?

Many Christian leaders throughout the ages, including the great reformer Martin Luther, have indicated that the pope personifies the Antichrist. I do not agree with this assessment. However, the papacy certainly does demonstrate the tendencies of the second beast, the false prophet. According to Revelation 13, the second beast will be powerful with authority to lead the leaders of the world toward one religion and ultimately to worship the image of the beast.

We must keep in mind that the endtime power structure is based primarily on deception and not on military power. This was visibly demonstrated by the media when it broadcast pictures of U.S. President George Bush, his wife Laura, and former Presidents Bill Clinton and George Bush Sr. on their knees facing the body of the dead pope. The President also had ordered all flags to be flown at half-mast. Significant, isn't it? Thus we see the invisible power of the papacy.

Although the Vatican does endorse the absolute truth of Holy Scripture, the Catholic Church simultaneously adds its own doctrine and then considers it divine, especially the teaching of papal infallibility. Therefore, only the Catholic Church has the intellectual, political and religious capacity to produce another Jesus, another spirit and another gospel.

The unifying power of the papacy is mind-boggling. Not only was this man honored for his ability to create unity among members of the world's religions and politicians, but he was also revered by

Churchianity and members of virtually all mainstream religions.

The False Prophet

It would indeed be a grave error to label any particular pope, the Vatican or the Catholic Church as the false prophet, because the office and the spirit of the false prophet include the entire world, particularly Churchianity.

I want to go one step further: If your life as a born-again Christian does not align itself with Holy Scripture, then you are a manifestation of the spirit of the false prophet.

When the word "church" is mentioned today, it is generally recognized as being the Roman Catholic Church. However, the Bible clearly identifies the Church as being any place where two or three people are gathered together in His name. Paul sent salutations to the saints, named them by name, and wrote: "with the church that is in their house" (1 Corinthians 16:19), and Colossians 4:15 reads: "and the church which is in his house." Therefore, the Church is made up of the fellowship of believers. The Church is not bound to an organization, but is in itself an organism. It is called the Body of Christ, and it is built upon the foundation of the apostles and the prophets with Jesus Christ Himself as the chief cornerstone. That Church is not subject to any nation or organization. It is vitally important that you belong to that Church.

When you belong to the Body of Christ, you will aim at a different target: not the things of the world, but the things that are in heaven: "For our conversation is in heaven; from whence also we look for the Saviour, the Lord Jesus Christ" (Philippians 3:20). Looking for and waiting for Jesus is a natural state of preparedness for the true Church. Our future is not here on planet Earth. We are not waiting and hoping for a better world. Our desire is the fulfillment of 1 Thessalonians 4:16-17: "For the Lord himself shall descend from heaven with a shout, with the voice of the archangel, and with the trump of God: and the dead in Christ shall rise first: Then we which are alive and remain shall be caught up together with them in the clouds to meet the Lord in the air: and so shall we ever be with the Lord."

Chapter 11

ANTICHRIST

As we have already mentioned, the Antichrist is the visible manifestation of Satan incarnate on earth. Man will create an image that will be worshipped by all people. Thus, it behooves us to take a closer look at this person, the Antichrist, because his masterpiece will be the Mark of the Beast.

"Little children, it is the last time: and as ye have heard that antichrist shall come, even now are there many antichrists; whereby we know that it is the last time. They went out from us, but they were not of us; for if they had been of us, they would no doubt have continued with us: but they went out, that they might be made manifest that they were not all of us" (1 John 2:18-19).

John is the only Bible author who used the word "Antichrist." The preceding verse reads, "And the world passeth away, and the lust thereof: but he that doeth the will of God abideth for ever" (verse 17). So we are concerned with two things: the temporary and the eternal. John wrote, "it is the last time," although that was almost 2,000 years ago. We must keep in mind that he was writing these words from a spiritual perspective. Everything we can realize with our five senses belongs to this world, which is temporary. But what we learn from Scripture is eternal.

The Antichrist and the spirit of the Antichrist know that he has only a short time; therefore, he must bring all of humanity into his bondage quickly. He is not doing that with weapons of war; rather, he presents it in a fashionable way so that people will voluntarily subject themselves to the desires created by the media inspired by Satan.

We need not blame the news media, the entertainment industry, the liberals, the humanists, the leftists, or any other group. The entertainment industry moguls keep track of who watches what. They actually present what people want. We already have discussed the media's role in the moral decline of the nations. But we must not overlook the fact that when the entertainment industry, for example, goes one step further to demoralize the viewers, then they can only do that if the people enjoy it, thus creating a vicious cycle. The media presents more brutality and more immorality in its movies and television programs because that is what sells that is what people want. Important for any business is that the people become hooked on its products. Success is based upon that level of achievement.

While this kind of approach is to be expected in

the world, we should be completely flabbergasted to see it also happening in the Church. Yet another Jesus is being presented in another gospel through the power of a false spirit and the people are enjoying it. The Apostle Paul wrote to the Corinthians about the substitute Jesus:

> But I fear, lest by any means, as the serpent beguiled Eve through his subtilty, so your minds should be corrupted from the simplicity that is in Christ... For such are false apostles, deceitful workers, transforming themselves into the apostles of Christ. And no marvel; for Satan himself is transformed into an angel of light. Therefore it is no great thing if his ministers also be transformed as the ministers of righteousness; whose end shall be according to their works (2 Corinthians 11:3, 13-15).

The Blessed Separation

The key event in this endtime scenario is the separation of those who have not been born again. They "went out from us" because "they were not of us." That is a blessed separation. This is the first non-ecumenical action initiated by those who could no longer identify with the true Church. They were not kicked out, but they "went out from us."

Doubtless this happened during the time when John wrote these words because he made a very personal appeal to "the little children." This is not a prophetic statement that would take place 2,000 years later, but it happened then and there: "Even now there are many antichrists."

John was concerned about the genuine believers who apparently were confused about those who had left the fellowship. But they were not real Christians; they were the product of the spirit of Antichrist. It is clear from this statement in Scripture that the spirit of separation was present in the Church, which means the fake ones could no longer stand in the presence of truth that was demonstrated by genuine believers in the Church.

Instead of Christ

Perhaps it is necessary at this point to explain that the word "Antichrist" means "instead of Christ." Antichrist is a substitute for the real Christ. Those who believed in the substitute Christ during John's time were the first anti-Christians. Although they named the name of Christ, called themselves Christians and seemed to follow the doctrines of the Bible, they actually did not belong to Jesus Christ.

When we speak about the preparation for the Mark of the Beast, we must keep in mind that this is not a new phenomenon. The Antichrist, the Mark of the Beast, and things of apocalyptic nature were just as real in the beginning of the Church as they are today.

Neither the Antichrist nor the Mark of the Beast has been revealed. Again, our desire is not to speculate about the Antichrist's identity, nor will we speculate about the type of technology that will be used for the Mark of the Beast. But all of these statements regarding the Antichrist and the Mark of the Beast make up one package; it applied to the Church in the beginning, and it applies to the Church in the final stages of the endtimes.

The Holy Spirit Exposes the Antichrist

John did not provide any further explanation about the Antichrist other than the statement recorded in 1 John 2:20: "But ye have an unction from the Holy One, and ye know all things." This obviously is the key to recognizing and separating the truth from a lie, darkness from light, and Christ from the Antichrist. The Holy Spirit teaches us all things: "But the anointing which ye have received of him abideth in you, and ye need not that any man teach you: but as the same anointing teacheth you of all things, and is truth, and is no lie, and even as it hath taught you, ye shall abide in him" (verse 27). The Holy Spirit abides with us forever. We are to abide in the teaching of the Holy Spirit.

The statement, "know all things...need not that any man teach you" may require a few words of explanation. It doesn't mean that we are not in any need of teaching, but it does mean that the Spirit leads us to distinguish between the truth and lies.

John did not reveal details as far as time is concerned, but the spiritual child of God sees the beginning and the completion: the same Spirit, the same doctrine, and not surprisingly, the same enemy.

When we speak about the preparation for the Mark of the Beast, we must deal with the subject in the same manner. Those who lived during John's time who had departed from the Church had not literally received the Mark of the Beast, but in a spiritual sense they had already been marked because they were not of the truth. They fell for a deception, a false christ, an imitation, the Antichrist.

The Warning

In view of the deception, the Church during John's time and today's Church should heed this warning: "Let that therefore abide in you, which ye have heard from the beginning. If that which ye have heard from the beginning shall remain in you, ye also shall continue in the Son, and in the Father. And this is the promise that he hath promised us, even eternal life. These things have I written unto you concerning them that seduce you" (1 John 2:24-26). Notice the words "abide," "beginning," and "continue." We are to abide from the beginning — that is, the moment we were born again of His Spirit and became eternal beings. Now we are to continue in the faith. Why? One word: seduction: "concerning them that seduce you." That is the spirit of the Antichrist, which was very much alive during John's time and is very much alive today.

How do we oppose seduction? Verse 27 answers: "But the anointing which ye have received of him abideth in you, and ye need not that any man teach you: but as the same anointing teacheth you of all things, and is truth, and is no lie, and even as it hath taught you, ye shall abide in him." Again we notice the word "abide." The Holy Spirit abides in us; it teaches us to differentiate between truth and lies, genuine and fake.

Dear friend, have you thanked the Father for the gift of the Holy Spirit? Without the Holy Spirit, we are in darkness, children of this world who have no hope and no future. But when we abide in Him who abides with us, then the precious Word becomes plain and open; we do not need signs and wonders, spectacular events or miracles. We simply believe that He is.

Waiting for Jesus

Did John wait for the coming of Jesus? Verse 28 answers: "And now, little children, abide in him; that, when he shall appear, we may have confidence, and not be ashamed before him at his coming." Note that he includes himself: "we may have confidence." He certainly believed in the imminency of the coming of Jesus Christ even in those days.

Therefore, waiting for Jesus separates us from the others who are waiting for a better time, less crime, greater freedom, more righteousness and many other things here on earth. In other words, if you are not waiting for Jesus, you are waiting for the manifestation of Antichrist. You are being prepared to receive the Mark of the Beast.

Who Is the Antichrist?

The Antichrist is Satan's masterpiece. He is a near-perfect imitation of Jesus Christ. He is the world ruler referred to in Scripture as the "son of perdition" (John 17:12; 2 Thessalonians 2:3); "the lawless one" (2 Thessalonians 2:8); the "king of fierce countenance" (Daniel 3:23); and a brilliant negotiator who will bring peace to the world.

Daniel offers more insight about the Antichrist and his kingdom in chapter 7:23: "Thus he said, The fourth beast shall be the fourth kingdom upon earth, which shall be diverse from all kingdoms, and shall devour the whole earth, and shall tread it down, and break it in pieces." The word "diverse" is repeated several times in this chapter. We notice that the fourth beast is not limited to one place, but "shall devour the whole earth." How will he do it?

> And his power shall be mighty, but not by his own power: and he shall destroy wonderfully, and shall prosper, and practise, and shall destroy the mighty and the holy people. And through his policy also he shall cause craft to prosper in his hand; and he shall magnify himself in his heart, and by peace shall destroy many: he shall also stand up against the Prince of princes; but he shall be broken without hand (Daniel 8:24-25).

Notice the words "destroy wonderfully"; "prosper"; "shall cause craft to prosper"; "magnify himself" and "by peace shall destroy many." He is the ultimate leader; he is the success story of the new

global world. Notice the words "peaceably," "flatteries" and "deceitfully" in chapter 11:21-24:

> And in his estate shall stand up a vile person, to
> whom they shall not give the honour of the king-
> dom: but he shall come in peaceably, and obtain
> the kingdom by flatteries. And with the arms of a
> flood shall they be overflown from before him, and
> shall be broken; yea, also the prince of the
> covenant. And after the league made with him he
> shall work deceitfully: for he shall come up, and
> shall become strong with a small people. He shall
> enter peaceably even upon the fattest places of
> the province; and he shall do that which his
> fathers have not done, nor his fathers' fathers; he
> shall scatter among them the prey, and spoil, and
> riches: yea, and he shall forecast his devices
> against the strong holds, even for a time.

The word "flatteries" continues to occur in verses
32 and 34. Verse 36 again testifies that he "shall prosper."

The Bible does not identify the Antichrist by name,
nor does it tell us that we should search for his identity. But one thing becomes clear: He is the most successful man on earth. The Chinese communists, the
Arab Muslims and the world's Churchianity will hail
this person as the messiah of the world, the great savior, a miracle worker, and the most benevolent man in
history.

Revelation offers additional information: "and all
the world wondered after the beast. And they wor-

shipped the dragon which gave power unto the beast: and they worshipped the beast, saying, Who is like unto the beast? who is able to make war with him?" (Revelation 13:3-4). Verse 8 says: "And all that dwell upon the earth shall worship him." We do well to take careful notice that this man and his system is global, not limited to a certain country or race of people. Finally, the world will have achieved peace and safety, but we know the Bible says that when they say peace and safety, sudden destruction will come upon them.

For those who try to identify the Antichrist, look for a nice guy, a person everybody will love, a politician unlike any other who will promise and fulfill and, as a result, will earn the adoration, even worship, from the world.

Chapter 12

RECEIVING THE MARK OF THE BEAST

We already determined that the definite identity of the Mark of the Beast is unknown to us and we will speculate in vain as to what it is and how it will be applied. In this chapter, we will highlight the Mark of the Beast as documented in the Bible.

The devil knows that children of God will receive a new name; thus, he must offer a substitute. Therefore, the implementation of the Mark of the Beast can only be successfully applied when the devil lulls people into believing he can offer them the real thing. People will think they are Christians and believe in Jesus Christ, but it will only be an imitation. They will accept the Mark of the Beast in order to belong to that family.

Before we proceed, there is one more issue we must highlight: the non-Christian world. Surely Muslims, Hindus, Buddhists, etc., will not become Christians, and by Christians I mean being identified as one belonging to Churchianity. However, the Bible does say that all who dwell on earth will worship the image of the beast. The question is how. Here we may use Daniel Chapter 3 to illustrate how this can and most probably will happen.

In that chapter, Babylonian King Nebuchadnezzar had an image built that was made out of gold. "He set it up in the plain of Dura, in the province of Babylon" (Daniel 3:1). Notice what was required to be a part of this first Gentile superpower: "Then an herald cried aloud, To you it is commanded, O people, nations, and languages, That at what time ye hear the sound of the cornet, flute, harp, sackbut, psaltery, dulcimer, and all kinds of musick, ye fall down and worship the golden image that Nebuchadnezzar the king hath set up. And whoso falleth not down and worshippeth shall the same hour be cast into the midst of a burning fiery furnace" (Daniel 3:4-6). Doubtless, this was an international group because the text says, "people, nation and languages." They were to worship the image or they would be killed. They were not required to reject their own idols, the gods they worshipped, or their own religions, but they were required to worship Nebuchadnezzar's manufactured image.

Translated into our times, Christians can remain Christians, Muslims will continue to be Muslims and the same will be true for all religions, but they all will come together for one specific reason: to worship the image of the beast.

This is the ultimate success of diplomatic deception, when all religions of the world will worship the image of the beast, with each one retaining its own gods and idols. Religion — which in the past was one of the major reasons for diversity, bloodshed and war — will be a major ingredient in unifying the world. Now the image of the beast, which is not connected to any specific religion, becomes the key factor of world unity.

Read Revelation 13:16-17 again: "And he causeth all, both small and great, rich and poor, free and bond, to receive a mark in their right hand, or in their foreheads: And that no man might buy or sell, save he that had the mark, or the name of the beast, or the number of his name."

Voluntarily Receiving the Mark

People are prepared to accept the Mark of the Beast. They want it and will voluntarily receive it. Following is a list of all the Scriptures in the book of Revelation that deal with the Mark of the Beast. This should confirm that people will voluntarily receive the Mark of the Beast.

• Revelation 14:9: "And the third angel followed them, saying with a loud voice, If any man worship the beast and his image, and receive his mark in his forehead, or in his hand." This is clear. It means people may or may not worship; they may or may not receive the Mark of the Beast. I see no evidence here that the Mark will be forced upon anyone.

• Revelation 14:11: "And the smoke of their torment ascendeth up for ever and ever: and they have no rest day nor night, who worship the beast and his image, and whosoever receiveth the mark of his name." Important also to note is that the Mark of the Beast comes in conjunction with worshipping the image. Obviously that means the ones who were deceived will actually agree with the Antichrist and the new global system of identification and worship.

• Revelation 15:2 (which reveals a different group of people that will not receive the Mark of the Beast): "And I saw as it were a sea of glass mingled with fire: and them that had gotten the victory over the beast, and over his image, and over his mark, and over the number of his name, stand on the sea of glass, having the harps of God."

• Revelation 16:2: "And the first went, and poured out his vial upon the earth; and there fell a noisome and grievous sore upon the men which had the mark of the beast, and upon them which worshipped his image." Worship and receiving the Mark go hand-in-hand. This will be judgment upon two categories of people: 1) those who have the Mark of the Beast and 2) those who worship his image. But we do not read anything about repentance, because they will still believe that they are on the right track, doing the right thing, worshipping the God of heaven (they think), but they will have actually been deceived.

• Revelation 19:20: "And the beast was taken, and with him the false prophet that wrought miracles before him, with which he deceived them that had received the mark of the beast, and them that worshipped his image. These both were cast alive into a lake of fire burning with brimstone." Clearly, those who receive the Mark of the Beast will have been deceived; they will not have been forced to take the Mark of the Beast. You can't make someone be deceived; it is always voluntary.

• Revelation 20:4: "And I saw thrones, and they sat upon them, and judgment was given unto them: and I saw the souls of them that were beheaded for the witness of Jesus, and for the word of God, and which had not worshipped the beast, neither his image, neither had received his mark upon their foreheads, or in their hands; and they lived and reigned with Christ a thousand years."

Worship or Death

We have now learned that martyrdom will be the only way to escape receiving the Mark of the Beast during the Great Tribulation. These people will be beheaded "for the witness of Jesus and for the word of God."

They will not participate in the global religion offered by Satan to the whole world. The Bible says that they "had not worshipped the beast, neither his image, neither received his mark upon the foreheads or in their hands." Therefore, it seems logical to presume that no one will survive the reign of the Antichrist. Those who refuse to receive the Mark of

185

the Beast will be killed. Now we come to a great problem: If all who refuse to worship the Antichrist will be killed, and those who take the Mark of the Beast will be destroyed, who are the people over whom the saints will reign "with Christ a thousand years?"

Name and Number

According to Revelation 16:2, the people are identified who will receive the Mark of the Beast and worship his image. This is reconfirmed in Revelation 19:20: "them that had received the mark of the beast, and them that worshipped his image." I fail to read of people who will receive the number of his name. We also read in Revelation 14:11: "who worship the beast and his image, and whosoever receiveth the mark of his name." To make this more clear let us reread Revelation 13:17: "And that no man might buy or sell, save he that had the mark, or the name of the beast, or the number of his name."

The KJV seems to reveal three groups: 1) those who will have the "mark," 2) "or the name of the beast," and 3) "the number of his name." All other translations I have studied indicate two categories: 1) the name of the beast and 2) the number of his name. Note also the previous verses we quoted in conjunction with the Mark of the Beast; no three categories are mentioned. Therefore, I must conclude that the Mark is expressed in the name of the beast and the number of his name.

Those identified who will receive the "name of the

beast" are unconditionally condemned. But those who receive "the number of his name" are not listed as condemned. Obviously, they will have done so for practical purposes of survival and not out of conviction. Therefore, I suggest the possibility that those who receive "the number of his name" will not be destroyed and will experience the return of Jesus Christ on the Mount of Olives. They will experience the implementation of the 1,000-year kingdom of peace.

That, however, does not mean they are saved. It is a mistake to assume that all who enter the 1,000-year kingdom of peace are saved. Saved people do not need to be ruled with a rod of iron. Israel, collectively, will be saved because Romans clearly states that after the fullness of the Gentiles has come in, "all Israel shall be saved" (Romans 11:26).

We must answer the two questions: 1) "Who will be left on planet Earth to enter into the millennium?" and 2) "Who are the nations over which the believers and the overcomers will rule?" No one will be left if all those who take the name and number of his name are destroyed. All who do not worship the image of the beast also will be killed. So who will be left on earth after Jesus returns?

I presented this issue in my first book, *How Democracy Will Elect the Antichrist*. Again I emphasize that the people who receive the number of his name and experience the beginning of the 1,000-year kingdom of peace are not saved.

Those who enter the kingdom of peace will still be unregenerate. For that reason, Christ and His Church will rule the nations "with a rod of iron." Why is that necessary? Because sin will no longer be tolerated, but instantly judged. This is evident from Isaiah 65:20: "There shall be no more thence an infant of days, nor an old man that hath not filled his days: for the child shall die an hundred years old; but the sinner being an hundred years old shall be accursed." The last sentence in the Hebrew translation reads: "and he who fails to reach a hundred shall be reckoned accursed." Saved people can never be accursed. All sinners will be eliminated at the end of the 1,000-year period.

This analysis is according to my understanding of the prophetic Scripture. I present this to the Church, and the readers may judge for themselves.

The Great Escape

There is an alternative to this understanding, namely, that multitudes will escape the clutches of the Antichrist. They will somehow hide during the Great Tribulation, subsequently escaping the Mark of the Beast. But that understanding seems to violate the repetitious use of the word "all" in Revelation 13:3,7,8,12,14,16: "and *all* the world wondered after the beast...and power was given him over all kindreds...And *all* that dwell upon the earth shall worship him...and causeth the earth and them which dwell therein to worship the first beast...And deceiveth them that dwell on the earth...And he causeth *all,* both small and great, rich and poor, free and bond, to receive a mark in their right hand, or in their foreheads."

If "all" does not mean "all" — with the exception of those who are deceived — then there is a great escape, a hiding away from the global power of the Antichrist.

Dangerous Interpretations?

I am aware that this interpretation may be dangerous because it could cause some to think they can accept the Mark of the Beast and still be saved, but that is definitely not the case because there aren't any second chances. If the Holy Spirit convicts you of your lost condition, then today is the day of salvation. If you deliberately postpone your decision, then you are in danger of remaining lost for all of eternity.

The Only Escape

Our task as children of God and servants of our Lord is to call people to repentance so that they will receive forgiveness based on the shed blood of the Lamb. Each one who decides to repent of his or her sins and follow Christ, and subsequently is born again, will take part in the great disappearance of the Church known as the Rapture. That is the only choice you have now: You can either say "yes" to Jesus or you can say "no" to Him. Therefore, let me admonish you with Scripture, "Today, if ye hear his voice, harden not your heart!" (Hebrews 3:7-8).

Chapter 13

THE INVISIBLE BATTLE

" While we look not at the things which are seen, but at the things which are not seen: for the things which are seen are temporal; but the things which are not seen are eternal" (2 Corinthians 4:18).

Another important issue in relationship to the Mark of the Beast is our battle in the invisible world. We must never be so naïve as to think that what we experience, hear or see has any relation to Bible prophecy. We already have dealt with the issue regarding God's time and have noted that for Him, a 1,000 years is like a day and a day is like a 1,000 years. In other words, the measurement of time as we perceive it has no relationship to God's time. When we realize this, we discover the reality of the invisible world: "The things which are not seen are eternal." With these facts in mind, let us now look at some of the issues relating to the invisible battle.

Ephesians 6:12 is one of the most neglected, mis-understood and wrongly interpreted verses in

Scripture: "For we wrestle not against flesh and blood, but against principalities, against powers, against the rulers of the darkness of this world, against spiritual wickedness in high places." This verse will help us better understand the preparation of the Mark of the Beast for the unbelievers and the preparation for the Rapture of the believers.

Note the words, "not against flesh and blood." Everyone is made up of flesh and blood but not everyone is our enemy! Our enemies are not people who worship Satan, nor are they atheists, agnostics, or those who oppose Christianity. The most obvious group today is the Muslims, who violently oppose the teaching of Christianity. But neither are they our enemies, because they are "flesh and blood."

Numerous organizations and movements have agendas that diametrically oppose Christianity, particularly the ones we call liberals — those who endorse abortion, same-sex marriage, etc. But even they are not our enemies, according to Scripture.

Madelyn O'Hara

I recall an experience we had in the beginning of our ministry in the 1970s. During that time there was much talk about Madelyn O'Hara, the famous atheist who made fun of any religion, especially Christianity. Christians took up arms to fight this perceived enemy. I recall the many letters we received requesting us to sign petitions, publish warnings in our magazine and participate in the fight against her.

Of course, we did no such thing. As a result, we were labeled as being "a ministry with no backbone," "standing for nothing and will fall for everything." We received a number of threats against our ministry in those days.

What were these people doing? They were fighting against flesh and blood! Madelyn O'Hara was a human being who traveled far and wide to deny the existence of God. Instead of warning against her, I thanked our heavenly Father for Madelyn O'Hara's testimony, because her very work proved the existence of God the Creator. You can't deny something that does not exist! Her denial of God's existence proved that she was deeply burdened in her soul and tried desperately to believe that there was no God.

Moral Activism

I could list countless experiences we have had since we began our ministry in 1968. We have been repeatedly urged by well-meaning Christians and political activists to get involved in the battle to fight against flesh and blood.

What is the result of Churchianity's fight against flesh and blood? Consider our nation as an example. The United States contains the largest Christian activity in the world. Although we make up only about 6 percent of the world's population, we are responsible for about 80 percent of the world's Christian literature, not to mention radio, television, film and other resources. Yet when we compare the United States with other countries, we quickly see that our fight with "flesh and blood" is not paying off.

We are the most criminalized country in the Western world. Our prison population is ten times higher per capita than in most European countries. Although the U.S. has the strictest laws and a very effective system of law enforcement, we still carry the sad title of world capital for pornography, illegal drug trade and other abominable activities.

Worst of all, however, is that our churched society has become the greatest destroyer of God's institution, the family. The U.S. is the undisputed leader in divorce, and that includes divorce in Bible-believing Christian marriages.

I realize that many will be offended by these truths but I need to record them in order to emphasize that fighting against "flesh and blood" results in Satan winning the victory. Our fanatical political involvement will weaken our spiritual ability to fight the real battle.

Deception of Self

Against what do we wrestle? We wrestle against "principalities, against powers, against the rulers of the darkness of this world, against spiritual wickedness in high places." In other words, our battle is against the invisible world, things we cannot see or identify.

Who rules the darkness of this world? Not presidents, prime ministers, chancellors or dictators! The rulers are the power structures of Satan and his host of demons. So the question is this: How can we fight against the invisible world?

Our battle requires self-denial. How did Jesus fight the devil? He denied Himself. We read in Luke 9:23-26:

> If any man will come after me, let him deny himself, and take up his cross daily, and follow me. For whosoever will save his life shall lose it: but whosoever will lose his life for my sake, the same shall save it. For what is a man advantaged, if he gain the whole world, and lose himself, or be cast away? For whosoever shall be ashamed of me and of my words, of him shall the Son of man be ashamed, when he shall come in his own glory, and in his Father's, and of the holy angels.

Furthermore, didn't Jesus plainly teach that we are to love our enemies? "But I say unto you, Love your enemies, bless them that curse you, do good to them that hate you, and pray for them which despitefully use you, and persecute you" (Matthew 5:44). These words need not be interpreted or analyzed by scholars; they are plain enough. Why then do we read in our Christian media countless statements totally centered on self:

- "we are fighting for freedom and democracy"
- "our battle is for justice"
- "we will fight evil and eradicate it"

This doctrine of devils, however, is very popular among the overwhelming majority of Christian authors, institutions, colleges and churches. The bottom line is always self; it's the diabolically inspired "I will" of Lucifer himself.

In contrast, the substitute church will always emphasize self-assurance, self-esteem, success, prosperity, health and wealth.

One of the most popular teachings sweeping across the land is the gospel of self. I received a note the other day with an article entitled "Learn to love yourself!" It lists five simple steps to show you that you are "priceless":

1. Accept yourself
2. Love yourself
3. Be true to yourself
4. Forgive yourself
5. Believe in yourself

Such teaching is producing unity in Churchianity. Interestingly, it corresponds with such Eastern religious practices as yoga, karate, acupuncture and a number of others, all for one expressed purpose: "So that you learn to love yourself!" That is the gospel of the false prophet proclaiming the Antichrist whom the world will honor, praise, adore and even worship as is documented in Revelation 13:8: "And all that dwell upon the earth shall worship him."

Preparing for the Mark of the Beast

The growing preparation for man's self-improvement will doubtless lead to the creation of a better world where people live together in harmony. Only through a positive impact upon the life of the overwhelming majority of people on planet Earth will the possibility be created for unity among the nations. In fact, it is amazing to see how generous, compassionate and concerned people become when natural catastrophes strike. They are called good, upright, honest, hard-working, tax-paying, God and country-honoring Americans. But from a biblical perspective, all of these wonderful attributes are summarized in Isaiah 64:6: "But we are all as an unclean thing, and all our righteousnesses are as filthy rags; and we all do fade as a leaf; and our iniquities, like the wind, have taken us away." Note carefully that this does not refer to the bad things we do, but of our "righteousnesses."

The Coming New Age Glory

From a human perspective, the new age will be absolutely glorious. Never before will man have gotten along so well with one another. There will be no conflicts between the nations. Mankind will be one great, global, happy and prosperous family.

Therefore, I venture to say that people will stand in line, happy to be waiting to receive the Mark of the Beast. They already will have been spiritually prepared for this glorious, peaceful instrument offered to all people. The Mark of the Beast will guarantee membership in this global society, and will include all rights and privileges.

The great tragedy is that the majority of

Churchianity hasn't the foggiest idea what it means to fight against "spiritual wickedness in high places." Subsequently, the prince of darkness has it relatively easy when it comes to confusing and seducing the masses, and using them for his purpose of world dominion.

The Silent Battle

So if we are to not fight against flesh and blood, then what is the real battle? I would like to answer this with the words of the late Dr. Wim Malgo, founder of Midnight Call Ministries: "Our greatest battle is not to fight." How do we know that that is the proper way?

The prophet Isaiah provided a description of this person: "He was oppressed, and he was afflicted, yet he opened not his mouth...as a sheep before her shearers is dumb, so he openeth not his mouth" (Isaiah 53:7).

Jesus was delivered to Pilate for interrogation 700 years after Isaiah wrote that prophecy, and we read: "he answered nothing" (Mark 15:3). The next two verses say: "And Pilate asked him again, saying, Answerest thou nothing? behold how many things they witness against thee. But Jesus yet answered nothing; so that Pilate marveled" (verses 4-5).

Jesus is our example. He is the Good Shepherd, the head of the Church and the One we should follow. Jesus won the greatest victory in all of history by standing still, and not defending Himself. Yet, He defeated death, hell and the devil. Because of His refusal to fight flesh and blood, He could later proclaim, "All power is given unto me in heaven and in earth."

Battle Preparation

Are we then not to fight the devil? Should we not oppose sin and corruption? Yes, we are, but here is the biblical way to do that: "Put on the whole armour of God, that ye may be able to stand against the wiles of the devil" (Ephesians 6:11). Note carefully, it does not say anything about fighting, attacking or beating, but simply "to stand." "Wherefore take unto you the whole armour of God, that ye may be able to withstand in the evil day, and having done all, to stand. Stand therefore, having your loins girt about with truth, and having on the breastplate of righteousness" (Ephesians 6:13-14).

My dear brothers and sisters, you don't have to fight the devil. Actually, you don't stand a chance if you do because you can't fight something that has already been defeated. You are making a mockery of Jesus' victory. Jesus defeated the father of lies on Calvary's cross when He cried out "It is finished." Are you trying to do better?

Our Real Battle

So, what must you do? Verse 18 answers: "Praying always with all prayer and supplication in the Spirit, and watching thereunto with all perseverance and supplication for all saints." Our first priority is not prayer for sinners, supplication for your government, or even for your family, but "for all saints." If you belong to the Church of Jesus Christ, then you are part of the Body of Christ and that supercedes all things on this earth. You are in the world, but you are not of the world. Realizing this fact will allow you to be placed under the spirit of the fear of God. Proverbs 9:10 says: "The fear of the LORD is the beginning of wisdom: and the knowledge of the holy is understanding."

Incidentally, that is the key to protection against the powers of darkness. In other words, we must in practice exercise our spiritual being.

The events that are taking place in our surroundings, in this country, or the world are of little significance to you as a spiritual person who is being opposed by principalities, powers and rulers of darkness of this world. If we only would realize what is happening in the invisible world, the things on this earth would become so insignificant that we would have little or no time for them. Then our energy, time and strength would indeed be invested in "praying always with all prayer and supplication in the Spirit." Our greatest concern should be the well being of the Body of Christ. Contributing towards that well being cannot be achieved through wrestling with flesh and blood. He who has an ear to hear, let him hear!

Chapter **14**

THE DEMON OF SENSATIONALISM

❝ And I saw three unclean spirits like frogs come out of the mouth of the dragon, and out of the mouth of the beast, and out of the mouth of the false prophet. For they are the spirits of devils, working miracles, which go forth unto the kings of the earth and of the whole world, to gather them to the battle of that great day of God Almighty" (Revelation 16:13-14).

That indeed is demonic sensationalism. It seems like the victory preparation for the world under the leadership of Satan. Imagine the entire world with all its armed forces proudly demonstrating their power. Flags raised, national anthems sung, speeches made...in unity against one tiny country, Israel.

This vision describes all of hell in an uproar, with the unclean spirits producing "miracles," the kind described in 2 Thessalonians 2:9: "Even him, whose coming is after the working of Satan with all power and signs and lying wonders."

201

Please keep this introduction in mind as we go into this chapter with the distinct intention of exposing deception through sensationalism.

It is important to notice that these unclean spirits will go forth "unto the kings of the earth." Who are these "kings?" On one hand, they are the rulers, the prime ministers, chancellors, presidents, dictators, etc., but on the other hand, they are the demonic powers that stand behind these political leaders.

Note the phrase "of the whole world." That means *all* people; the entire human race will be involved.

The Bible clearly states that the prince of darkness is the god of this world and the overwhelming majority of people is following in the footsteps of the father of lies. That is the earthly view.

But there is more. The last sentence of that verse says: "to gather them to the battle of that great day of God Almighty." As human beings, we cannot fight against God Almighty, because He is not a physical, visible entity. Therefore, this is a spiritual view of this great confrontation.

Also, notice in Revelation 17:14: "These shall make war with the Lamb." Again, this is impossible because physical beings cannot fight the Lamb of God. People are only capable of waging war against other people. We have done that right from the beginning, when Cain slew his brother Abel.

Armageddon

What is "the battle of that great day of God Almighty?" It is the Battle of Armageddon: "And he gathered them together into a place called in the Hebrew tongue Armageddon" (Revelation 16:16). We have just read that God will gather the nations to battle, yet in Revelation 16:14 we read: "For they are the spirits of devils, working miracles, which go forth unto the kings of the earth and of the whole world, to gather them to the battle of that great day of God Almighty." Is the initiator of the Battle of Armageddon God or the devil? Revelation 16:14 plainly shows that demonic forces are the initiators, but verse 16 states that God does the gathering of the nations. The entire world — under the leadership of Satan and manifested by the three unclean spirits — opposes God the Almighty. (These spirits proclaim themselves God, but the God in heaven tells them where to go: Israel.) That's God's physical point of contact with planet Earth. God came down from heaven and became flesh and dwelt among the people in the land of Israel. There, He fought the greatest battle in all of history — but the battle was non-sensational, it involved only one innocent person being nailed to the cross and crying out, "It is finished." That's why God will lead the nations — under the leadership of Satan — to Israel to execute His judgment upon the nations who refuse to receive forgiveness of their sins through the shed blood of Calvary's Lamb.

If we analyze these Scriptures from a demonic perspective, however, then our theology of a literal battle involving all nations in a specific location falls apart. Demons cannot fight literal battles with planes, tanks, bombs and guns. But doubtless, like all other wars in history, the demons will be behind the nations fighting the various wars. The Battle of Armageddon may not occur in the way that it has been sensationalized in recent years in books and movies. But that does not change the fact that there will be a war, although it will be fought with different means.

The preceding verses reveal the preparation for this war:

> And the sixth angel poured out his vial upon the great river Euphrates; and the water thereof was dried up, that the way of the kings of the east might be prepared. And I saw three unclean spirits like frogs come out of the mouth of the dragon, and out of the mouth of the beast, and out of the mouth of the false prophet. For they are the spirits of devils, working miracles, which go forth unto the kings of the earth and of the whole world, to gather them to the battle of that great day of God Almighty (Revelation 16:12-14).

Here we see that "the spirits" will initiate the gathering of the nations. They will perform "miracles" to lead the world against God.

Destructive Judgment

Next comes the battle:

> And the seventh angel poured out his vial into the air; and there came a great voice out of the temple of heaven, from the throne, saying, It is done. And there were voices, and thunders, and lightnings; and there was a great earthquake, such as was not since men were upon the earth, so mighty an earthquake, and so great. And the great city was divided into three parts, and the cities of the nations fell: and great Babylon came in remembrance before God, to give unto her the cup of the wine of the fierceness of his wrath. And every island fled away, and the mountains were not found (Revelation 16:17-20).

This is judgment that leads to destruction. This is not a description of a battle as we imagine it with guns, tanks, planes and missiles. Something will happen there that is unprecedented; therefore, it must not be compared with previous battles or methods of war. We are dealing here with God's judgment upon a rebellious world.

No Repentance

It is significant to note that this judgment from God does not result in repentance, but in blasphemy. Scripture states:

> And the kings of the earth, and the great men, and the rich men, and the chief captains, and the mighty men, and every bondman, and every free

man, hid themselves in the dens and in the rocks of the mountains; And said to the mountains and rocks, Fall on us, and hide us from the face of him that sitteth on the throne, and from the wrath of the Lamb...And the rest of the men which were not killed by these plagues yet repented not of the works of their hands, that they should not worship devils, and idols of gold, and silver, and brass, and stone, and of wood: which neither can see, nor hear, nor walk: Neither repented they of their murders, nor of their sorceries, nor of their fornication, nor of their thefts...And men were scorched with great heat, and blasphemed the name of God, which hath power over these plagues: and they repented not to give him glory. And the fifth angel poured out his vial upon the seat of the beast; and his kingdom was full of darkness; and they gnawed their tongues for pain, And blasphemed the God of heaven because of their pains and their sores, and repented not of their deeds (Revelation 6:15-16; 9:20-21; 16:10-11).

This destructive war will come directly from God and will target a godless world.

Watching and Waiting

What is the alternative to the battle of God Almighty? To answer that, we must read Revelation 16:15: "Behold, I come as a thief. Blessed is he that watcheth, and keepeth his garments, lest he walk naked, and they see his shame." We are to watch and to keep our garments. These garments are not our own; they are garments of righteousness that have been washed in the blood of the Lamb. Thus, the way to avoid the Battle of Armageddon is to be ready, watching and waiting for our Lord's return.

Here it is helpful to also read Revelation 7:14, an important message John the Revelator received: "These are they which came out of great tribulation, and have washed their robes, and made them white in the blood of the Lamb." They will be the ones who are watching and waiting for the Lord.

Those of us who belong to Jesus have received the robe of righteousness and we are to keep it spotless. Can that be done? Absolutely, but only through Jesus Christ and the power of the Holy Spirit.

What will happen if we do not watch? "Lest he walk naked and they see his shame." For that reason the Apostle John admonished: "And now, little children, abide in him; that, when he shall appear, we may have confidence, and not be ashamed before him at his coming" (1 John 2:28).

Sensationalism: Tool of Antichrist

What will precede the Battle of Armageddon is important to understand. That's why this chapter is titled "The Demon of Sensationalism." Let us now take a closer look at this matter.

The world must be one in order to accomplish "the battle of the great day of God Almighty." At this time, it seems virtually impossible for the world to unite. But the devil and his demons must create this unity in order to lead the world to rebel against the Creator. Therefore, the demonic world must present something to humanity that is real and believable. Lying signs and wonders must become visible. But how can that be accomplished?

Terrorism

Just before I started writing this chapter, the bombing of the London public transportation system was in the headlines. The internet and radio reported one story after another about this horrible event. Sinister minds had to be at work to do this much damage and to take this many lives.

While it was terrible that approximately 50 people were killed (at the time of writing), it was not a major catastrophe compared with the murder and bloodshed taking place daily in many cities around the world.

For example, firearms claim the lives of more than 25,000 people each year in the United States. That means 25,000 American terrorists (murderers) have caused 25,000 casualties. Divide that by 365 days, and we're talking about roughly 70 people who are killed each day. Yet these 25,000 terrorists (murderers) don't make the headlines unless they are excessively cruel or murder several people at the same time. Otherwise, the reports don't go any further than the local news.

You probably won't read about a murder that occurred 100 kilometers from your home town, because it's not considered newsworthy.

Consider the events of September 11, 2001, when the most horrendous terrorist act ever launched against the United States resulted in the deaths of about 3,000 people. The savagery was accomplished by young, demonically inspired Muslim men, mostly Saudi-Arabian citizens, who committed suicide in order to kill as many Americans as possible. The events of that day caused a global sensation. Everyone knows what happened on 9/11. This type of sensationalism is capable of uniting people everywhere.

The Result of 9/11 Sensationalism

What was the result of this sensational terrorist attack? It moved the world one step closer to total control. Who in his right mind would oppose our intelligence bureaucracy gathering information about individuals with the intention of diverting the next terrorist act? Since the overwhelming majority of the population is made up of "good" people, we don't even think twice about volunteering our personal information to confirm our "innocence." After all, this newly required security is aimed to catch criminals — in this case, terrorists. The government may have all the information it wants about me if that will help to catch the one who has evil intentions. Never mind that hundreds of thousands of murders are committed year after year.

We gladly overlook the fact that now the government has more information about us than ever before. But for the sake of security and in our fight against terrorism, we must bring the sacrifice and permit the government to intercept our mail and our e-mail, and even listen to our telephone conversations. We cannot deny that now the avenue is open for the government to legally step into our private lives.

This is the result of sensationalism; not because of the 70 people who are murdered each day by American terrorists, but because of the sudden, sensational impact the Muslim terrorist attack had on the United States.

That is part of the process of preparing the world for the coming Mark of the Beast through sensationalism.

Chapter 15

WHY THE MARK OF THE BEAST MUST COME

Jesus used the phrase "end of the world" on several occasions. For example, Matthew 28:20 states: "Lo, I am with you always, even unto the end of the world. Amen."

The disciples understood the term "end of the world." That is why they asked, "What shall be the sign of thy coming and the end of the world?" (Matthew 24:3).

How did Jesus answer that question? "Take heed that no man deceive you." With that statement He shifted the priority from the realization that the world would come to an end through a very personal issue of deception

The End of the World

What does the end of the world mean? For the believer, the end of the world will be a new beginning; it is the beginning of eternity. But for unbelievers it will mean eternal separation from God and His glory.

Second Thessalonians 1:7-9 says: "And to you who are troubled rest with us, when the Lord Jesus shall be revealed from heaven with his mighty angels, In flaming fire taking vengeance on them that know not God, and that obey not the gospel of our Lord Jesus Christ: Who shall be punished with everlasting destruction from the presence of the Lord, and from the glory of his power."

Deception of Success

Why does the world refuse to believe in the Gospel of the Lord Jesus Christ? We find the answer in the word "deception."

Believers know that their existence on earth is temporary, and we look forward to eternity. The unbeliever, on the other hand, only has hope here on the earth. Thus, unbelievers look forward to a better time, a more peaceful society, a happy family. They want to live in comfort and prosperity. Most would agree those are noble goals; therefore, any means by which this goal can be attained will receive total support from the population.

Therefore, the two groups of people, the believers and the unbelievers, must be separated. Although both groups seem identical, one already has the invisible mark of the Holy Spirit: they are new creatures in Christ. The other group is being prepared to receive the Mark of the Beast.

Be Separate

The Church is instructed to be separate: "Wherefore come out from among them, and be ye separate, saith the Lord, and touch not the unclean thing; and I will receive you" (2 Corinthians 6:17). Hebrews 7:26 explains why: "For such an high priest became us, who is holy, harmless, undefiled, separate from sinners, and made higher than the heavens." Churchianity seems to go in the direction that leads one closer to the world instead of further away from it.

But separation is clearly taught in the Bible. Israel's separation repeatedly is documented: "For wherein shall it be known here that I and thy people have found grace in thy sight? is it not in that thou goest with us? so shall we be separated, I and thy people, from all the people that are upon the face of the earth" (Exodus 33:16). Leviticus 20:24 says, "But I have said unto you, Ye shall inherit their land, and I will give it unto you to possess it, a land that floweth with milk and honey: I am the LORD your God, which have separated you from other people." Israel's uniqueness lies in its separation from the nations of the world: "For thou art an holy people unto the LORD thy God: the LORD thy God hath chosen thee to be a special people unto himself, above all people that are upon the face of the earth" (Deuteronomy 7:6).

Furthermore, we read in 1 Peter 2:9: "But ye are a chosen generation, a royal priesthood, an holy nation, a peculiar people; that ye should shew forth the praises of him who hath called you out of darkness into his marvellous light." We are in the world, but we are not of the world: that is the difference ordained by God.

Separation requires identity. At this time, the world is separated. Nations are divided from other nations by their languages, culture, traditions and customs. To create a united world, Satan must compel people to eliminate borders and surrender their national identities so that the world will become one happy global family.

Movement of People Control

Almost daily we hear news reports about illegal workers. Most of us think that this is strictly happening in the United States, but that is far from the truth. The majority of the world's legal and illegal immigrants and workers are flooding into Europe, but the problem is also occurring in all countries of the world.

An article from the *Times of India* states:

> The government said it proposed to issue smart cards and set up a 24-hour helpline for migrant Indian labor to protect them from "exploitation."
>
> "We will be introducing an electronic emigration card (smart card) to protect vulnerable workers from exploitation by unscrupulous agents, employers and emigration staff and eliminate cor-

ruption in the system," minister for overseas Indian affairs Jagdish Tytler said here at an interactive session with Forum of Financial Writers.

Tytler said the chip in the smart card will contain all the information about the worker like where the person is employed, nature of job, contract, salary, etc. In case they face any problem, all this information will be utilized for the benefit of the worker ("Smart Cards for Emigrants on Anvil," 21 June 2005).

India, the world's largest democracy, has begun to take stock of its population, in this case, to protect laborers from being exploited. But the bottom line remains the same: registry of individuals. Doubtless, that, too, is part of the preparation for the Mark of the Beast.

Citizenship Identity

We know from Scripture on certain occasions the Apostle Paul used his Roman citizenship to protect himself from abuse. In one case, he protested his punishment by asking: "Is it lawful for you to scourge a man that is a Roman, and uncondemned?" (Acts 22:25). What was the proof? Paul's word! The captain asked him, "Art thou a Roman?" He answered: "Yea."

Now compare that to today. When you travel abroad, you are not asked about your citizenship. The only identification that proves who you are is your passport. The official looks at your passport then places it in an electronic scanner to confirm that it is valid. In other words, the officer does not believe your word or the passport itself; he bases approval solely on the results of the scan. Thus, the ultimate proof of your identity and nationality is the machine called the computer.

Identity Theft

To better understand the complexity of issues relating to identity, particularly identity theft (IT); consider the following excerpt from *Financial Times*:

> Once a sleepy IT backwater, identity management has been thrust into the spotlight over the past few years.
>
> More and more companies, alarmed by the escalating incidence of identity theft, have come to understand the importance of protecting the integrity of digital information held about individuals.
>
> According to a recent report prepared by Nemertes Research, the US based research firm, 38 percent of all enterprises cite identity management as a top-funded security initiative.
>
> Recent figures from industry analyst Morgan Keegan show that the global identity management market is worth about $4.8bn and is estimated to grow to about $10.7bn in 2007.
>
> "Today, business success is dependant on fast and easy access to information," notes IBM. "However, the internet-enabled rise of e-business

has dramatically increased the scope and number of an organization's constituencies, making information management, user management, and security management complex and expensive."

"Identity management systems are critical for organizations," adds Bruce Schneider, a leading US security expert. But Mr. Schneider, who founded Counterpane Internet Security, a recognized leader in managed security services, adds: "They're less about security and more about process efficiency. When someone moves around in an organization — gets hired, fired, promoted or goes on vacation — their access to resources changes. Identity management systems allow administrators to deal with their information accesses in one place."

Sun's Ms. Gates argues that identity management really emerged as an issue at the end of the 1990s when it became clear that networked information and resources were growing at a phenomenal pace.

"It was virtually impossible for companies to keep up using traditional manual methods, not to mention completely unaffordable," she says. All of this was of course complicated by the fact that over the past few years, the emphasis for most corporate IT departments has been doing more with less.

To be effective companies need to share a common federated identity management system architecture so a group of IT companies led by Sun Microsystems formed the Liberty Alliance. The Alliance set out to define three basic specifications including the Liberty Identity Federation Framework (ID-FF), which allows for a single sign-on, account linkages, anonymity, affiliations and various options for the exchange of metadata ("Managing the digital identity crisis" by Paul Taylor, July 27, 2005 FT.com).

This process is one of the many ingredients that will promote the implementation of total control through the Mark of the Beast.

Counterfeit Problem

Virtually every type of document can be counterfeited; that is one of the biggest problems facing officials today. How can they circumvent that problem? Through the biometric passport, which features additional identifying information (such as fingerprints) in order to make it nearly impossible to falsify identification documents.

Nevertheless, there is no such thing as foolproof identity, in spite of the most sophisticated technology available. There always will be criminals who will detour the legal avenues and invent and implement their own devices to beat the system.

Each day, countless technicians and scientists are working hard to come up with a foolproof and effective identification system. Remember, we are speaking of preparation for the Mark of the Beast and not the actual Mark. Thus the question: How can the world come up with a foolproof identity system?

We may search far and wide, but we won't find a more accurate system than what is recorded in Scripture: "And he causeth all, both small and great, rich and poor, free and bond, to receive a mark in their right hand, or in their foreheads: And that no man might buy or sell, save he that had the mark, or the name of the beast, or the number of his name" (Revelation 13:16-17).

In summary, the process of identifying people will continue until the Mark of the Beast has been implemented. But we do not know what the Mark of the Beast will be, and there is no need to speculate because the development of technology, particularly in electronics, is exploding. However, we can say with certainty that all of the preparations that are being made now will lead towards the goal of the preparation for the Mark of the Beast!

Tribulation and Prosperity

Scripture records what the world's reaction to the coming destruction will be:

> For all nations have drunk of the wine of the wrath of her fornication, and the kings of the earth have committed fornication with her, and the merchants of the earth are waxed rich through the abundance of her delicacies... How much she hath glorified herself, and lived deliciously, so much torment and sorrow give her: for she saith in her

heart, I sit a queen, and am no widow, and shall see no sorrow...And the kings of the earth, who have committed fornication and lived deliciously with her, shall bewail her, and lament for her, when they shall see the smoke of her burning...And the merchants of the earth shall weep and mourn over her; for no man buyeth their merchandise any more...The merchants of these things, which were made rich by her, shall stand afar off for the fear of her torment, weeping and wailing, And saying, Alas, alas that great city, that was clothed in fine linen, and purple, and scarlet, and decked with gold, and precious stones, and pearls!...And cried when they saw the smoke of her burning, saying, What city is like unto this great city! And they cast dust on their heads, and cried, weeping and wailing, saying, Alas, alas, that great city, wherein were made rich all that had ships in the sea by reason of her costliness! for in one hour is she made desolate (Revelation 18:3, 7, 9,11,15-16,18-19).

These Scriptures reveal that at first, society will be successful, prosperous and wealthy. After that prosperity is removed, weeping and wailing will result.

Consider the phrases such as "waxed rich through the abundance of her delicacy," "glorified herself, and lived deliciously," "shall see no sorrow," "kings of the earth," "lived deliciously," "merchants," "were made rich by her," "clothed in fine linen," "purple," "scarlet," "decked with gold," "precious stones, and pearls," "were made rich all that had ships," "by reason of her costliness."

These speak of super success and unlimited prosperity — in other words, exactly what is going on today. Never before has mankind been so rich, lived in such luxury, or had such an abundance of material blessings and unimaginable comfort. If you don't believe it, just ask someone who is 70 or 80 years old. He or she will testify of extreme hardship, excessive physical labor and mostly uncomfortable living conditions. Even better, read the history books: Not even royalty could dream of the luxuries we take for granted today. In ancient times, the kings could not have the wide selection of food that is available now; nor could they enjoy the comforts of conveniences such as electricity, air conditioning and long-distance communication. How about travel? Carriages drawn by sweaty horses traveled at slow speeds over terribly dusty, rocky roads. Going a mere 20 or 30 kilometers was a major undertaking. So much for the good old days!

When judgment comes and the world sees the destruction of its material goods, one thing will be lacking: repentance. That is the greatest tragedy of all and that is also the tragedy of our day, when materialism has become the idol of our time.

Fornication

One word stands out in Revelation 18:3: "fornication." The Bible often uses that word when describing Israel's apostasy, which they demonstrated by idol worship. What kind of idols does the world worship

221

today? Two prominent ones are success and materialism.

Revelation 9:20-21 provides another record of the worshipping of idols through materialism: "And the rest of the men which were not killed by these plagues yet repented not of the works of their hands, that they should not worship devils, and idols of gold, and silver, and brass, and stone, and of wood: which neither can see, nor hear, nor walk: Neither repented they of their murders, nor of their sorceries, nor of their fornication, nor of their thefts."

Personality Cult

Some may say that no one in his right mind would worship another person. I disagree. It happens all the time. Dedicated support of any "hero," whether it is a movie star, politician or athlete, is the first step toward worshipping. Take, for example, a talk show host who commands yearly earnings of hundreds of millions of dollars. Where does the money come from? From people who support the show. The extreme support of these idols is mind-boggling! People so idolize celebrities that they even buy the products and services they endorse. This practice occurs not only in business but also in politics and religion. Politicians are no longer elected based on qualifications, but on popularity. Unfortunately, this is also the case in religion. The "package" of a preacher becomes more important than the words he speaks. The personality cult has elevated many preachers to celebrity status. It may be good to have dedicated followers, but popularity can put religious leaders at risk of taking the liberty to reinterpret or misuse Scripture.

Idolatry is an important part of the success of the New World Order, as documented in Scripture.

Worshipping

Take note that receiving the Mark of the Beast goes hand in hand with worshipping: "If any man worship the beast and his image, and receive his mark in his forehead, or in his hand...who worship the beast and his image, and whosoever receiveth the mark of his name...men which had the mark of the beast, and upon them which worshipped his image...which he deceived them that had received the mark of the beast, and them that worshipped his image" (Revelation 14:9,11; 16:2; 19:20). This is man's destiny. He definitely will worship the image of the beast. Preparation for the acceptance of worshipping man is well in progress. Otherwise, global corporations would not pay hundreds of millions of dollars to celebrities to endorse their products or services.

Slowly but surely we see the development towards the worshipping of the ultimate idol, the image of the beast.

Global Unity

Let's confirm that this is global: "And he exerciseth all the power of the first beast before him, and causeth the earth and them which dwell therein to worship the first beast, whose deadly wound was healed" (Revelation 13:12). You can't get more global than "the earth and those who live there." This is not limited to Israel or the Middle East; it encompasses the whole world, all of humanity.

The world is dominated by democracy, with only a few pockets of resistance. From an economic perspective, no one can oppose the European system of social capitalism, which has now taken hold of communist China.

But religiously there seem to be insurmountable obstacles. Just think for a moment about Churchianity and Islam. For all practical purposes, it is impossible to unite these two religions. Can you imagine Christians going to a mosque on Friday and Muslims coming to church on Sunday? At this time, it may indeed seem impossible but it will happen because it is documented in prophetic Scripture. We can't get around the statement, "and all that dwell on the earth shall worship him."

To the question of when it will happen, we have one answer: when the Church of Jesus Christ is present on earth. The Church is the light of the world and the salt of the earth, which means that as long as there is light in the world, the powers of darkness will not be able to manifest themselves to the extent they would like.

The Great Disappearing

There will come a time when suddenly, and in the twinkling of an eye, all believers on planet Earth will be raptured into the presence of the Lord into the clouds of heaven. First Thessalonians 4:16-17 says: "For the Lord himself shall descend from heaven with a shout, with the voice of the archangel, and with the trump of God: and the dead in Christ shall rise first: Then we which are alive and remain shall be caught up together with them in the clouds, to meet the Lord in the air: and so shall we ever be with the Lord."

The World After the Church

What will happen to this planet after the Church has been taken away? We do not know because the Bible does not provide any details about how the world will react. However, one thing we are absolutely sure of is that the Rapture will unite the world more closely than ever. Just imagine what might happen when countless people suddenly disappear from this planet without any explanation!

A word of caution: We must not confuse the Church with Churchianity. Churches are located on practically every street corner in the United States. Church buildings are fewer and farther between in Muslim countries; thus, on the surface, you could say there is no evidence of the Church's existence in that place. But that would be a great mistake because Jesus promised to build His Church, and He is doing that. Even in countries such as Saudi Arabia, Iran, Afghanistan, and other places, the Church is alive and well although it is not visibly manifested.

Communist China holds to the prevailing philosophy that religion is poison, and it should be forbidden. Now, however, it is evident that the Church of Jesus Christ in that nation is rapidly growing.

I would venture to say that the number of believers from countries we never thought the Church existed in will be surprisingly high, while countries considered "churched" will be surprisingly low. In other words, after the Rapture, churches will be filled with worshippers, and religious activities among Muslims, Hindus, Buddhists, etc., will continue. But because all nations will report the disappearance of its citizens, there will be unprecedented and widespread fear — a binding element for the nations.

The Mark for Security

The world will want to know more about the people who disappear. Their questions inevitably will lead to answers that point directly to the Mark of the Beast.

Religion, whatever kind, is socially acceptable, particularly since the demise of the Soviet Union. Religion will become so strong that it will take the upper hand in politics and economy. After the Church is raptured, terrorism, nuclear weapons, and other threatening issues will vanish because the greatest concern will be the mystery of the vanishing people. That will be the adhesive binding the nations together. They will focus their attention on an unknown enemy who snatches people without explanation. At that point, it seems logical that the Mark of the Beast will be available for all people who desire peace and security.

Let's read the passage again:

> And he exerciseth all the power of the first beast before him, and causeth the earth and them which dwell therein to worship the first beast, whose deadly wound was healed. And he doeth great wonders, so that he maketh fire come down from heaven on the earth in the sight of men, And deceiveth them that dwell on the earth by the means of those miracles which he had power to do in the sight of the beast; saying to them that dwell on the earth, that they should make an image to the beast, which had the wound by a sword, and did live. And he had power to give life unto the image of the beast, that the image of the beast should both speak, and cause that as many as would not worship the image of the beast should be killed. And he causeth all, both small and great, rich and poor, free and bond, to receive a mark in their right hand, or in their foreheads: And that no man might buy or sell, save he that had the mark, or the name of the beast, or the number of his name (Revelation 13:12-17).

The whole world will be religiously united, and worship will be directed to a man and his image because he will be the only one with an explanation for the great disappearance. He will guarantee that no more people will disappear. In order to implement that promise, all people must be registered, which means they will "receive a mark in their right hand, or in their foreheads." Life will be impossible on planet Earth because no one will be able to buy or sell any longer without the Mark.

Finally, the world will live in peace and security. There will be no more fighting between the nations. There will be no more hatred and jealousy. The world's population will confidently proclaim that it has peace and safety. But that will suddenly change. The Scripture says: "For when they shall say, Peace and safety; then sudden destruction cometh upon them, as travail upon a woman with child; and they shall not escape" (1 Thessalonians 5:3).

CONCLUSION

     " And I saw as it were a sea of glass mingled with fire: and them that had gotten the victory over the beast, and over his image, and over his mark, and over the number of his name, stand on the sea of glass, having the harps of God" (Revelation 15:2).

There are many different aspects of the preparation for the Mark of the Beast. In this book, we have considered the difference between the Mark, which is the beast's name, and the number of his name. Scripture clearly marks a distinction between the two. Furthermore, some will receive the Mark or the number on their right hands, while others will receive it on their foreheads. Again, we want to make it clear that at this time, no one knows what the Mark or the number will be, nor do we know how it will be implemented or applied. We do know, however, that it will happen. We also know that the intellectual elite, as well as the population at large, will demand peace and security for the entire world. Therefore, no nation can stand by itself. Independence will not be tolerated.

Some nations, such as North Korea, Iran, and Cuba, are isolated to a certain degree. The rest of the nations, regardless of their government affiliations, are marching to the beat of Roman democracy. They are intermingling to the extent that there is no longer a clear distinction between their individual societies. Therefore, we can say with reasonable assurance that the world has become one. It stands to reason, therefore, that a global government with the capability of enforcing law and order must come into being. That, however, will only be accomplished when all people have been properly registered and identified. That's what the Mark of the Beast and the number of his name is all about.

Foreshadows of Things To Come

Let's briefly analyze the development of the world's culture, which is energized by three categories of popular activities:

1. Working
2. Shopping
3. Identity

Working

Man has had to work by the sweat of his brow in order to put bread on the table, clothes on his back and a shelter over his head. All that changed with the

Industrial Revolution. Food, clothing and shelter, provided primarily through agriculture, have become a minor concern for people in the industrial world. Only between 1-2 percent of the workforce of progressive nations is involved in agriculture. Working for material possessions has become the primary goal of most people. Although it would seem that people today would have more time on their hands than ever because of the many time-saving and work-reducing machines in use, people are actually working more than ever before. Work has become so precious that spending quality time together has become virtually non-existent for many families.

We, the so-called free people of the world, require the comfort of shops being open seven days a week, 24 hours a day. As a result, people are working longer hours, and are spending less time at home. Retirement age, which the bulk of the population used to eagerly anticipate, is becoming a thing of the past. In the U.S., older people often continue to work until they literally drop dead. We have become a free people who willingly subject ourselves to the bondage of work until the end of our lives.

The Bondage of Buying

Becoming virtual slaves to the boss has become the norm. Money is the reward for that excessive amount of work. The obsession with work, then, naturally leads to an obsession with materialism. Christians immerse themselves in this culture of workaholics and quite naturally become shopaholics. How much time do you spend each week shopping? Should one hour be sufficient? How about two, three, or five? Recent research revealed that most Americans spend an average of 15-20 hours a week shopping. What are they shopping for? In most cases, they are shopping for things they really don't need! But precious family time is sacrificed for the sake of possessing material things.

Family time isn't the only casualty of this preoccupation with working and excessive materialism. The spiritual implications are even greater. Since so much time is being consumed with work and shopping, many people have little time left to heed the advice Moses gave in Psalm 90:12: "So teach us to number our days, that we may apply our hearts unto wisdom." Martin Luther translated this verse as follows: "Teach us to remember that we must die, so we may attain wisdom." Many lives revolve around work, money, and buying; yet, the Bible clearly teaches that preparing for eternity by watching and waiting for the coming of Jesus should be our priority. Life on earth is temporary and each moment should be spent with eternity in mind.

Our Lord Jesus spoke about the daily activities that would be taking place in the endtimes: "But as the days of Noe were, so shall also the coming of the Son of man be. For as in the days that were before the flood they were eating and drinking, marrying and giving in marriage, until the day that Noe entered into the ark" (Matthew 24:37-38). It seems strange that Jesus mentioned only the everyday activities we continue to perform even in this century. We eat and drink, we marry and give our children into marriage, but one thing is lacking: preparations for eternity. The Bible says, "And as it is appointed unto men once to die, but after this the judgment" (Hebrews 9:27).

The Bondage of Identity

A group of people is described in Revelation 15:2 who will not participate in the global identity process. They enjoy victory. The time will come when the Mark of the Beast will be offered as the remedy for the world's ills, and will be gladly accepted by the majority of the population.

But who in his right mind would accept this Mark on his right hand or his forehead? The key word is "preparation." Abraham, the father of all believers, made preparations so that a nation could be formed for God's specific purpose. That nation had to be prepared to bring forth the Messiah of Israel and Savior of the world. At this point, the Church is being prepared for heaven. We read in Revelation 19:7: "Let us be glad and rejoice, and give honour to him: for the marriage of the Lamb is come, and his wife hath made herself ready."

Satan must mimic this preparation; therefore, he will set up the entire world to worship the image of the Antichrist, which will be accomplished with total control through the Mark of the Beast.

Identity Preparation

We have already discussed how identity was established during Paul's time: a person's word was accepted as truth. Paul simply said that he was a Roman citizen and his word was believed. Such is no longer the case. Today, formal forms of identification are the only accepted verification of a person's identity.

Although the public is generally not in favor of a so-called identity card, everyone has numerous forms of identification. Social Security numbers, bank account numbers, credit card numbers and others all aid in the identification of a person.

But even these formal identification documents cannot always accurately identify a person; some forms of identification may be counterfeit. Thus, a foolproof system of identification must be established. According to the Bible, that will be the Mark of the Beast, which will remain with the person from birth until death. Preparation for it has been going on for many years, not only in the scientific field, but also on the commercial level — from the names and numbers proudly displayed on athletes' uniforms to the prestigious designer labels featured on clothing.

Not long ago, I tried to buy a baseball cap but could not find one without a logo advertising a manufacturer. I needed the cap to keep the sun off my head, not to promote a certain brand name. Yet I was virtually forced to become an endorsement for one of the companies. And in 1995, I bought a new car and stunned the salesman by asking how much his dealership would pay me to display its name on the trunk of my car. His answer, of course, was, "Nothing." Instead, I would have to pay the dealership money if I wanted to have the name removed. Doubtless, even the public's willingness to buy into endorsements and name-brand promotions is just another step towards preparation for the Mark of the Beast.

Tattoos

Tattoos once were reserved for members of a lower level of society, and were particularly identified with those who led lifestyles of drinking and immorality. Today, tattoos have become a fashion statement, as millions have marked their bodies for life.

Entertainment stars and sports idols in particular are leading the nations towards accepting permanent tattoos in order to express certain endorsements and ideas. Thus, the stars and idols become the objects of worship.

Creation Moments, the well-known two-minute radio broadcast headed by Ian Taylor, has offered the following information about tattoos:

> Dr. William Cardasis, a Michigan criminal psychiatrist, sees a possible link between criminal behavior and tattoos. In his study of 55 patients at a maximum security hospital, Dr. Cardasis has found statistical links between sociopathic behavior and the tendency to wear tattoos. He found that patients with tattoos were much more likely

to have no regard for the rights of others, behave impulsively and lie and steal with no remorse. Another study of cadavers in New York city showed that the bodies of teen drug addicts had twice the number of tattoos compared to the general population. One tattoo artist told the press that he refuses to tattoo the face, neck or hands. He pointed out that some people consider tattoos in these places to be "serial killer territory." Dr. Cardasis adds that simply having a tattoo doesn't mean one is a criminal — that depends on what the tattoo means to the person wearing it.

Getting a tattoo is a permanent commitment to the symbol represented by the tattoo. Believers should have a permanent commitment only to Jesus Christ.

Time and space do not allow for additional documentation, but by now the reader should have realized that the world today is definitely being prepared for a total identity system referred to in Scripture as the Mark of the Beast.

Some of modern science's fantastic achievements are also preparing the world for the Mark of the Beast, as is the world's desire for peace and security. One would have to be blind not to see the progress towards this end! For example, due to the so-called fight against global terrorism, people are willing to reveal more and more information about themselves for the sake of establishing peace and maintaining security. In reality, these measures are leading to total security, which will be sealed with the Mark of the Beast. When that time comes, most will not think twice about accepting the Mark. People all over the world are already pre-programmed to accept the Mark of the Beast through the bondage of work, the bondage of shopping and the bondage of identity.

The Only Escape

There is only one way out of the system of total control that will be implemented with the Mark of the Beast, and that is through faith in Jesus Christ, who accomplished and perfected salvation on Calvary's cross when He poured out His blood for the payment of sin. Acceptance of this free gift of salvation enables us to hear the words with our spiritual ears: "He that hath an ear, let him hear what the Spirit saith unto the churches; To him that overcometh will I give to eat of the hidden manna, and will give him a white stone, and in the stone a new name written, which no man knoweth saving he that receiveth it" (Revelation 2:17).

NIMONA

WITHDRAWN

NOELLE STEVENSON

HARPER TEEN

An Imprint of HarperCollinsPublishers

HarperTeen is an imprint of HarperCollins Publishers.

Nimona
Copyright © 2015 by Noelle Stevenson
All rights reserved. Manufactured in China.
No part of this book may be used or reproduced in any manner whatsoever
without written permission except in the case of brief quotations embodied in
critical articles and reviews. For information address HarperCollins
Children's Books, a division of HarperCollins Publishers,
195 Broadway, New York, NY 10007.
www.epicreads.com

ISBN 978-0-06-227822-7 (paperback) – ISBN 978-0-06-227823-4 (trade bdg.)

The artist used Adobe Photoshop to create the digital illustrations for this book.
Typography by Erin Fitzsimmons
21 SCP 15 14 13 12
❖
First Edition

To all the monster girls

CHAPTER 1

But I'm a huge fan of your work!

You're Ballister Blackheart, the biggest name in supervillainy!

You're an inspiration!

Yes, well, I don't need a sidekick.

Oh come on! EVERYONE has a sidekick these days.

I can't have some KID following me around all day.

I'm not a kid.

I'M A SHARK!

AAAAHH

Oh yeah, I forgot to mention I'm a shapeshifter.

Yes, you might have mentioned that.

Well, I suppose I can see how that would be useful.

Fine, you're hired. Welcome aboard.

YESSSSS

END OF CHAPTER ONE

CHAPTER 2

we were friends once. Heroes in training.

We were the two most promising heroes the Institution had ever seen.

until the day of the joust.

We'd never been pitted against each other before.

I knocked him clean off his horse.

It was a fair victory.

but Ambrosius hates to lose.

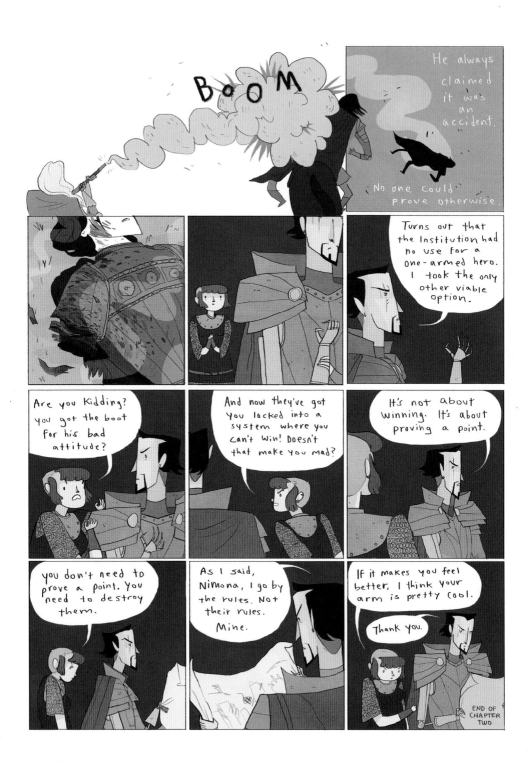

CHAPTER 3

FSS SSHHH

You know I could've infiltrated this place by myself in like ten seconds, right?

I'm not sending you out by yourself on your first heist. Consider this a test run.

Which one of these science things do you need again?

Poke

Don't touch anything. These are very volatile substances.

Ack

HALT, YOU VILLAINS! UNHAND THAT SCIENCE!

Fsssh

Goldenloin! I should've known you'd show up!

Why are you still surprised after all this time?

Shhh

I see you have a squire now! How nice for you, Ballister

Ambrosius, this is my new sidekick, Nimona.

YEAH AND YOU'RE GOING DOWN, GOLDENLOIN!

Well, she's certainly... Spunky.

Oh yeah, I'll show you spunky, fancy man.

Can I kill him now?

No.

Charming.

She grows on you.

14

LIVE

EXPLOSION AT LABORATORY

...is believed to be the work of renowned supervillain Ballister Blackheart. The number of casualties has not yet been confirmed...

INCOMING CALL

((( )))

DIRECTOR

Institution of Law Enforcement & Heroics

Some heist you pulled today, Blackheart.

What do you want?

The body count seems... uncharacteristic of you.

It didn't go according to plan.

You don't say.

Have they found any survivors yet?

Your sidekick? She didn't make it out. We made sure of that.

Then it was your people who set off the self-destruct!

We reacted to a potential threat.

She was just a kid!

That's none of our concern.

16

What kind of person blows up a building to kill one kid? You're a monster.

I'm not a monster.

I'M A SHARK!

AAAAHHH

HA HA HA HA HA

N-Nimona?

HA HA HA HA HA HA HA

DAMN YOU, NIMONA!

Hey, Boss! How ya doing?

You let me think you were dead!

You liiiike me, you were worriiied

You little...

Where are you?

At the Institution headquarters! They don't know I'm here.

Get back here, NOW.

Yeah, okay.

Can I bring all these TOP SECRET plans I found?

Yes! Yes! Just get out of there before they catch you!

You got it, Boss.

And don't EVER do that again.

Hey! You're not authorized to be in here!

Oops, gotta go!

NO NIMONA will you stop doing that!

AAHH

END OF CHAPTER THREE

CHAPTER 4

20

Yeah, but they worked for the Institution. You know, the same people that ruined your life?

The security guards didn't ruin my life!

No, Goldenloin did. And you won't even kill him!

No one's gonna take you seriously if you're too afraid to kill anyone.

LIVE

KINGDOM IN SHOCK

Now you've got their attention!

Everyone's waiting to see what you'll do next!

LIVE

SIR GOLDE

Who's the villain, and who's the sidekick here?

If you're going to stay, you need to listen to me.

Fine, but you need to actually give me something to do.

sip

Fair enough. We need to cooperate. we need to work as a team.

I will admit that that was some pretty quick thinking in there on your part.

So do I get to help you lay out the next evil plan?

Yes, if you promise to show a little more restraint.

Deal!

POUNCE

You're really good at that.

Thanks!

Where did you learn to do that?

How does it work?

I've heard of animal shapeshifters and face-changers, but nothing like this.

What's your story, anyway?

Aw man, do I HAVE to do the backstory thing? It's kind of a downer.

'Course, I bet you love downer stories, don't you?

Just tell me.

Fine.

It all started when I was six years old...

I lived with my parents in a tiny village. You know, super normal and boring stuff.

But we were always getting attacked by the raiders from the west.

They'd come without warning, pillaging and burning everything.

I wanted to fight them, but I was only six, and there wasn't a lot I could do.

Then one day I was gathering berries in the woods when I came across a hole in the ground.

HELP

Hey! You okay down there?

Alas, I am a poor old woman who has fallen down into this hole.

I am also a witch.

If you help me out, I will give you a magical gift.

If I get you out, can you make me strong enough to defeat the raiders from the west?

Hmmm

I know! I will turn you into a dragon. Then you can fly down and carry me out.

Really? Turn the six-year-old into a dragon? That was her idea?

Just listen to the story, okay?

26

Anyway, it sounded like a good idea at the time.

So she cast the spell and everything went according to plan...

...I became a fearsome dragon.

I carried the witch to safety...

...and saw her on her way.

I was excited to show the village my new dragon's shape, and how strong I had become!

But when I got there, they weren't exactly glad to see me.

The witch had forgotten to show me how to change back, or even how to speak.

I had to run away and find a cave in the woods to hide in.

I spent the next few weeks attempting to change back.

I don't get it. The witch turned you into a dragon — why were you able to become other animals?

The spell was slippery. She wasn't a very good witch.

Well, I'd guessed that much from her brilliant plan of "get out of the hole by turning the six-year-old into a dragon."

Will you please shut up about that?

Finally, I was able to transform back into myself.

I ran home as fast as I could to show my parents what I could do.

But when I got back, I found that the raiders had already come. Everyone from my village was dead, including my parents.

sip

So, yeah, kind of a downer, like I said.

What did you do after that?

Oh, you know, I just kind of wandered.

shelter wasn't a problem.

neither was finding food.

That's about it, really.

yes, come in, sir Goldenloin.

INSTITUTION OF LAW ENFORCEMENT AND HEROICS

I've been expecting you.

I was hoping you could explain all this to me.

Artist's rendering

It wasn't MY fault. Ballister's new sidekick broke the rules.

I didn't think she'd be such a problem. She's only a child, after all.

Dead

heart

Tell me, how did a child bring about the destruction of our finest research facility right under your very nose?

END OF
CHAPTER FOUR

33

CHAPTER 5

But how does your shapeshifting WORK? It doesn't make any sense.

It's magic! Can't you just accept it and move on?

No.

Ha, of course not.

"I'm Ballister Blackheart and I only believe in SCIENCE!"

AUGH

Don't do that! It's weird!

Don't do that! It's weird!

Nimona, I swear, if you don't turn back RIGHT NOW—

SsssSSCIEEEEENCE

Ha ha! You're so easy to mess with.

I can fire you anytime I want, you know.

Sure, Boss.

Drat this door.

What's wrong with it?

Nothing, it's just very high security.

I've got to enter a series of very precise entry codes, which in turn activate the retinal scanners.

Once the retinal scan is verified, the voice-activation software goes online, and—

KRRASH

Not high security enough for me!

This is coming out of your paycheck.

see, that right there. you just altered your own mass. That's IMPOSSIBLE.

Tell that to your door!

Fine, so it's magic. What CAN'T you do? What are the rules?

Hmm.

Well, I can't turn into anything inanimate, for one.

Unless I want to BE inanimate, if you catch my drift.

Two, I can only turn into creatures that actually exist.

I can turn into any person, real or made-up, but that's harder.

36

CLANK

Nimona?
Are you okay?

I'm not going to run any tests.

Did...did someone else..?

Ooh! What's that?

Does it KILL PEOPLE?

CAN I TRY IT?

DON'T TOUCH THAT

TIME TO SNOOP THROUGH THE INSTITUTION'S STUFF!

Let's see what they consider "top secret plans," shall we?

Aw, these aren't secret plans! It's just a bunch of gibberish!

What a rip-off!

It's encoded.

And that's— good?

They wouldn't be encoded unless they had something to hide.

And you can crack it?

I think so.

SYSTEM ON

Cool.

RUNNING PROGRA

40

Woah.

What?

Jaderoot? The Institution's using JADEROOT?

What? WHAT'S JADEROOT?

It's a very rare, VERY poisonous plant, and it's pretty much only used in dark sorcery.

It's extremely corrosive and notoriously hard to control.

The Institution outlawed it a long time ago.

And yet these plans suggest that they've somehow got a large amount of it.

What are the plans FOR?

It seems they're trying to formulate a material that can store the jaderoot's poison without dissolving.

And judging by the size of these containers, that's a LOT of jaderoot.

If it's so rare, then where are they getting it all?

That's what I'm worried about.

If they're growing it themselves, they risk contaminating the entire kingdom's crops!

Crops? You're worried about the CROPS?

If it starts poisoning everyone's food, then yes.

Good point.

Not to mention whatever they're planning on DOING with all this jaderoot.

So you're not crazy, huh? The Institution really IS up to no good.

You thought I was crazy?

No, no, crazy in a GOOD way! Evil mad scientist kind of thing!

Just stop.

sip

Communications to Director.

INCOMING CALL

This had better be important, Rudy.

Turn on the news, Director. Channel six.

What's going on?

...these documents suggest that the Institution has been hoarding large quantities of a substance known as jaderoot...

SCANDAL!

SECRET DOCUMENTS LEAKED

...a rare and deadly poisonous plant commonly associated with dark magic, and which the Institution itself has banned.

44

Should we shut it down?

If we cut it off now, they'll know we panicked.

SECRET DOCUMENTS REVEA

We'd only lend it credibility. Let it run its course.

Get a squad to the station and apprehend that anchorwoman as soon as it goes to commercial.

DIRECTOR!

SECRET DOCUMENTS REVEALED

Is this TRUE?

Calm yourself, sir Goldenloin. Of course it isn't true.

How do you explain it, then?

SECRET DOCUMENTS REVEA

Simple.

It's Blackheart.

45

46

48

49

LATER...

This movie is absurd.

It makes no logical sense and the production values are appalling.

Gah!

Are you really scared of this?

You can take on a whole squadron of guards by yourself, and THIS is what scares you?

Well maybe if they'd been UNDEAD guards, it would have been a different story!

I don't understand what's so scary about zombies.

Reanimating the dead isn't hard, but they make TERRIBLE minions.

They can't move quickly and they fall to pieces in a matter of days.

Will you just watch the movie?!

AAAIIIII!

SPLORTCH

NYARGH

GLOMP

Oh come on! That is NOT what intestines look like!

SHUT UPPPPP

51

Well, that was a waste of two hours.

Nimona?

zzz

Nimona, I need to go to bed.

tug

sigh

clip

click

END OF
CHAPTER FIVE

CHAPTER 6

55

ONE WEEK EARLIER

Whatcha making?

If you're going to come in here, GLOVES and GOGGLES.

grumble

CLATTER CRASH

Goggles. Gloves.

Now are you going to tell me what you're making?

It's the next phase of our plan.

Yes! Phases! Evil potions! This is what I'm talking about!

CAREFUL

Apples planted, SIR!

Good. Now we wait.

For how long?

The toxin is time released. The effects won't become apparent for at least a few weeks.

Aw, boring.

We have to make absolutely sure no one traces it back to us.

In the meantime...

...how would you feel about robbing a bank?

POSITIVELY! I FEEL POSITIVELY ABOUT ROBBING A BANK!

I thought you might.

HIS MAJESTY'S ROYAL TREASURY

Hello, sir! Are you here to make a deposit?

Not quite.

We're here to make a withdrawal.

67

Out of the way! Let me through!

What's going on in there?

Blackheart's robbing the bank, sir. We had to evacuate.

All right, with me, men. We're going in.

Sir, he's got— some kind of MONSTER with him...

A little girl disguised as a monster. Don't tell me you're AFRAID.

Sir—

—the roof.

RRAAAAAUGH

69

RAAAAAAAAUGH

AAAH   AAAH   AAH

Sir Goldenloin to headquarters. Requesting immediate backup. We need archers in the bank square NOW.

You two, with me. The rest of you, wait for backup.

But sir, the dragon—

She's a DISTRACTION. Meanwhile Ballister is helping himself to as much gold as he can carry.

Now's our chance! GO!

FOOOOOM

OOF

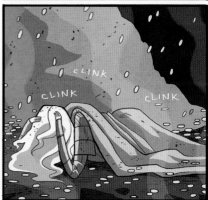

CLINK

CLINK

CLINK

Blackheart.

Hello, Ambrosius.

RAAAAAUUGH

what, are you Robin Hood now?

No. I'm a supervillain.

I know you are, Boss.

Aim for the wings. Just bring them down. I want them both ALIVE.

VRRRRRMMM

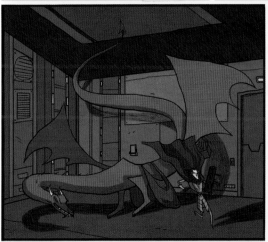

Haha oh man! That was awesome!

It went off without a hitch! And look at all this loot!

Ah— Nimona—

What?

Oh.

80

This is all my fault. I never should have let this happen.

Boss, I said it's FINE.

It's not like I didn't know it would be dangerous.

Did you though? Did you REALLY?

I know this all seems like a big game to you, but the Institution doesn't play around.

They won't pull their punches just because you're young.

I'm not EXPECTING them to!

I appreciate your concern, but I've been looking out for myself for a long time.

So don't baby me, okay?

I just don't want you to get hurt!

WILL YOU CHILL OUT?

No one ever got killed with one little arrow!

Actually, they do. That is kind of the PURPOSE of arrows.

And you need to stay off of that leg.

Aw, SERIOUSLY?

You're going to take it easy until it heals.

But what about all the evil plans!

It wouldn't hurt to lay low for a while.

UUUGGHH

So I'm stuck here with YOU until my leg gets better?

Afraid so.

Well, what's there to do around here, anyway?

Well, here we have World Domination; it builds strategy skills — you can play as a dog, a boot, or a trebuchet.

Bewilder builds language and observation skills...

I said I wanted to play VIDEO games.

Video games are a waste of time.

And board games AREN'T?

Why do you even have these? No one lives here but you!

I used to have some henchmen. Game night was a big hit.

Henchmen? What happened to them?

I can't work with mercenaries. It's impossible to build trust when they only care about their paychecks.

Oooh. Lemme guess. The Institution paid them off?

I don't want to talk about it.

World Domination, huh? I call the Scottie dog!

YES! a ten!

...eight... nine... ten!

Landing you in the Enchanted Forest, which is MY domain.

600 gold, please.

My scottie dog will not pay your tyrannical toll!

Nimona...

He rallies the oppressed woodland creatures and organizes a revolt!

It just so happens I am a just ruler and greatly admired by all my subjects.

Squirrels scale the walls of the castle and bears batter down the gates!

Bloody chaos ensues!

The Enchanted Forest is ours!

Flick

I'm taking the 600 gold anyway.

HIGHWAY ROBBERY!

Plus another 600 for damages.

FOOOOOsh

That was fun! What do you want to do next?

HIS MAJESTY'S
HOSPITAL
MEDICAL CLINIC

I've never seen anything like this, Doctor.

Four cases in the last week alone!

They're not responding to any treatment we've tried.

We've run every test — but I don't know what to make of the results.

We don't know what's causing it. The patients have no ties to each other.

AUTHORIZED PERSONNEL ONLY

Do you remember that news report? The Institution's secret stash of Jaderoot, poisoning the Kingdom's crops?

But the Institution debunked that...

QUARANTINE

Yes... but suppose it's true?

Angry crowds congregate outside Institution headquarters as rumors of a jaderoot-related plague mount...

Four cases have been reported so far. The Institution has yet to comment...

RIOTS BREAK OUT

This is a disgrace.

Due to your incompetence, Blackheart and his new ward are running CIRCLES around us.

INTSTITU

What would you have me do? Stop the peasants from getting sick?

This is not the time for smarm. You KNOW what you have to do.

DIRECTOR

Get rid of the sidekick.

By any means necessary.

I swear I will see them both captured and brought to justice...

Do I have to spell everything out for you?

RIOTS ERUPT

DISPOSE OF the sidekick.

What?

I'm not going to kill a little girl!

This is a matter of keeping your job. You think we can't replace you in an instant?

If this situation escalates any further, we will be forced to take drastic measures.

and your friend Blackheart WILL go down with her.

Blackheart is NOT my friend.

Right, archnemesis. of course.

And if you want him to REMAIN as such, you'll do as I say.

END OF
CHAPTER SIX

87

CHAPTER 7

...Kingdom is in panic after the outbreak of a mysterious disease, rumored to be linked to experiments carried out by the Institution...

Meanwhile, Villain-at-large Ballister Blackheart's recent bank heist has caused mass withdrawals, forcing authorities to freeze all accounts...

LOOK WHAT I GOT YOU!

What's this?

I nicked it at the bank! Figured it would suit you!

C'mon, Boss, just picture it! When we've won, you'll be King, and I'll be your champion!

I never said I wanted to be King.

Who did you think was gonna take over after we ousted the Institution?

Or did you just not think that far ahead?

89

Did you take the bandage off?

What? Oh.

Wha- it's healed already?

Not just healed... it's completely GONE.

Yeah, well, I heal really fast. It's a shapeshifter thing.

After FOUR DAYS?

Why didn't you mention this before?

FORGOT!

≡ BING ≡

INCOMING CALL

((( )))

SIR GOLDENLOIN

What do YOU want?

I need to talk to you.

Alone.

In person.

Can you meet me at the Antlered Snake tonight?

How stupid do you think I am?

It's not a trap, you have my word.

Your word is worth a lot, is it?

The institution doesn't know about this, okay? I just want to talk.

We're talking now.

PLEASE, Ballister. It's important.

I'll buy the drinks.

...Fine.

Seven o'clock.

BOOP

Sigh

Nimona, I'm going out.

But what about dinner?

Just put mine in the fridge.

scoot

Remember when we used to come here every day after training?

I remember.

Well, I'm here. What do you want?

Where's your sidekick?

Is THAT what this is about?

Is she here?

She might be. You'd have no idea, would you?

I'D have no idea...

You've got to get rid of her.

Is that so? And, uh—

WHY WOULD I DO THAT.

The Institution is very displeased—

Yes, that was the idea.

Ballister—

The Institution is ordering me to KILL your sidekick.

Killing Children now, Goldenloin?

Is that what heroes do these days?

Do you really think I want to do it?

What makes you think you CAN?

She'd eat you alive if I'd let her.

You Know how powerful the Institution is.

Just send her away, Ballister. She'll be safe, and things Can go back to normal.

CLANK

Normal, is it?

You gave up normal at the joust.

CLK

94

I can't believe you're still hung up about that.

It was a long time ago, you know.

Besides, it was an ACCIDENT.

I bet you've said that so many times you've started to actually believe it.

It WAS!

It's just the two of us here, Ambrosius. You don't have to lie.

wh—I'm not—everyone knows what happened that day! You're the only one who can't accept it!

Can't you just admit it, just this once?

you blew up my arm because you couldn't stand that I was better than you.

YOU WERE NEVER BETTER THAN ME!

97

BEEP

FSS SHH

Hey! You're home!

I put your dinner in the fridge like you said.

Whoa, what happened?

Did you get in a fight without me?

Tell me where they are! I'll mess their faces up!

BOSS?

I'm going to bed.

END OF CHAPTER SEVEN

CHAPTER 8

SHUF

SCIENCE EXPO TODAY

BRILLIANT MINDS FROM ALL OVER THE LAND TO EXHIBIT AT KINGDOM'S ANNUAL FAIR

BEEP

What's this about?

Well, you seemed really depressed last night, so...

I thought some science would cheer you up!

You LOVE science!

We can't go to a big public event like this, Nimona. We're the two most wanted criminals in the Kingdom.

I thought of that!

You're gonna need to put on this fake beard.

SCIENCE EXPO

ROBOT FIGHT

This beard itches.

Nimona, I really don't think this is going to fool anyone.

Well, it won't if you keep messing with it!

And my name's GREGOR.

Clearly I'm the only one taking this disguise thing seriously.

If we get caught it's YOUR fault.

Hey, this was your idea.

I haven't been here in years.

I used to dream about one day having my own booth here.

Ha, NERD.

So where should we...

Ooh! Churros!

105

Carry me!

Hey!

Nimona, I'm not going to carry you.

Oh please, I carry you all the time!

And it's GREGOR.

Fine. But can you turn into something less ...heavy?

It's rude to comment on a lady's weight.

Is anyone looking?

No, you're fine.

Okay, that works.

Hello! I see that my Anomalous Energy Enhancer has caught your eye.

Well, I do like green glowing things.

I'm Dr. Meredith Blitzmeyer. Here's my card!

Ah. Yes. And I'm—Gregor.

So what does it do?

Well, right now, it... glows green.

That's it?

It's a new technology.

But this green glow does not come from electricity, nor flame, nor bioluminescence, nor any energy source hitherto known to man!

It needs no fuel, and its light will persist indefinitely!

Mm-hmm.

I understand your skepticism. I'm the only one researching anomalous energy, and this is all I have to show for it.

Anomalous energy?

It's based on a theory of my own invention!

I have made the journey over the mountains to the lands beyond, where the great sorcerers still practice their craft.

I observed their methods and noted that they seemed to draw their power from an invisible, apparently infinite source.

I theorized that there must be a vast field of energy that surrounds us all, but is only made detectable under very specific circumstances.

I dedicated myself to re-creating those circumstances scientifically!

This humble device, good sir, is the first step to reconciling science and magic!

Okay. Okay. They've definitely seen me. We need to get out of here.

huf huf

you Know what would be REALLY helpful?

IF YOU WERE ANYTHING OTHER THAN A CAT RIGHT NOW.

HISSSSSS

SWIPE

what are you saying, you're STUCK?

111

114

116

Hey—
You okay?

Ngghhh.

WHAT THE
HECK WAS
THAT?!

SHHHH.
Can you get us
out of here?

Yeah, damn straight
I can. Hang on.

117

CRASH

Will you calm down?

NO.

That didn't go as well as it could have, but it's okay now.

You don't GET it!

I have NEVER lost my powers. I DON'T get STUCK.

It is NOT okay.

what if the Institution finds out about this machine, huh?

They're not going to find out!

you're not alone anymore, you know.

I can help you. I won't let them get to you.

I DON'T NEED YOUR HELP, OKAY?

I HAVE NEVER. NEEDED. ANYONE'S. HELP.

KRRRNCH

Do you know how many people have said they wanted to HELP me?

NIMONA. STOP IT.

THUNK

Sorry about your kitchen.

Guess that'll come out of my paycheck too, huh?

END OF CHAPTER EIGHT

In today's news, six new patients were admitted to His Majesty's Hospital yesterday with reports of unpleasant and mysterious symptoms, bringing the total number of cases to twenty-three.

BREAKING NEWS

A link has been suggested between the illness and the Institution's supposed experimentation with the deadly substance jaderoot.

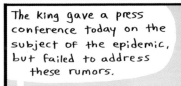

The king gave a press conference today on the subject of the epidemic, but failed to address these rumors.

Citizens are advised to avoid contact with infected parties, and examine all food for peculiar qualities before consuming it.

See that all infected parties are brought in for medical attention immediately.

And please remember to remain calm.

Nimona.

I know something happened to you. Something you're not telling me.

You don't have to tell me if you don't want to.

I trust you, you know. And you can trust me.

You know that, right?

BOSS.

It's fine, okay? Just let it go.

...Okay.

Are you hungry? I thought maybe we could order a pizza.

Sure.

Any particular toppings you want?

Nah, you pick.

Sardines it is, then.

Don't you DARE put sardines on that pizza.

Blackheart is past the point of being controlled. I want him out of the picture.

I'm telling you, he can still be useful to us!

That isn't your call.

You're already asking me to kill a young girl. If the public finds out you're sending me out on assassinations...

The public's opinion is not a priority right now.

If Blackheart dies, he'll be a hero for the commoners!

Arrest him, pin the poisonings on him...

Really, Goldenloin, do you fancy yourself sly?

Your motivations are quite transparent. I KNOW what the nature of your relationship was.

I made it clear at the time that I disapproved.

If your fixation on him has impeded your ability to do your job, then he truly has outlived his usefulness.

We'll find you a new nemesis.

Perhaps you will be more competent without Blackheart as a distraction.

I won't kill him.

If you demand I kill the girl, I'll do it — but I won't kill him.

Very well.

Guarantee the termination of the sidekick, take Blackheart into custody, and he will live.

Do we have an accord?

Yes, Director.

Good. Come this way. I have something for you.

You're clearly outmatched the way things are now, so let's even the field.

Shock-absorbent plating, robotically enhanced performance, electrical stun units in the gauntlets. It should be quite sufficient to subdue a half-mechanical man and a little girl.

You'll select a team to go with you. They'll be similarly outfitted.

I don't want any mistakes this time.

Should I lead an attack on his fortress?

It would be unwise to stage the conflict on his own turf.

We need to draw him out. Engage him on our own terms.

A trap? Ballister won't fall for that. He's too paranoid.

Hmm, perhaps.

It would not surprise me if he had become a little...overly confident these days, however.

Do they really think that this will appease people?

I don't know, I think we could all use a little fun.

This is just asking for trouble, if you ask me.

Boss, we have a problem.

What is it?

Goldenloin's not here.

He's got to be. He's on the poster!

Well, he's not in the program.

ROSTER

Keep an eye out.

Will do.

Where's the powdered sugar got to?

Wait here, I'll go get more.

Can't imagine where it went...

POW
SUG

Found it!

Enjoy!

On one side, knight errant Sir Coriander Cadaverish!

And on the other, representing the Institution— Sir Mansley Girthrod!

BOOOOO
BOOOOOO
BOOOO

Any sign of Blackheart yet?

None yet, Director.

He'll show, I'm sure of it.

What's going on over there?

Ma'am?

Unbelievable.

People
of the Kingdom.

My name is
Ballister Blackheart,
but I'm sure you know
that already.

You may think of
me as your enemy, but
I have only ever fought
against the Institution,
not against you.

Your true enemies are
the ones who have
beaten you down and
kept you in compliance
through fear.

They took your
children and raised
them as soldiers. They
mongered war at the
expense of their
people.

They've locked
us into a system
where they hold
all the power.

In return, they
promised you
safety, but they've
broken that
promise.

In their
quest for
war, they've
endangered
the very
people they
swore to
protect.

They took away
your power.

It's time to
take it back.

138

I've traced the signal of Blackheart's transmission.

It's coming from the communications terminal back at headquarters.

Attempting to access security cameras.

Security cameras have been disabled. Guards on duty not responding.

He's definitely there.

Do you hear that, Goldenloin?

Copy that, Director.

Get in there and TAKE HIM DOWN.

As to the rest of you, get this crowd under control.

By any means necessary.

Nimona, how's it going out there?

DOWNLOADING

All going according to plan. How about on your end?

I'm almost done.

That's enough, Blackheart.

Turn around.

Slowly.

Boss? Are you okay? What's going on?

Well, I found Goldenloin.

Boss!

FZZT

CRAP.

141

WARNING. FULL LOCKDOWN IN PROGRESS.

CLANK CLANK CLANK

CLANG

Ha! It's another trap! A DOUBLE trap!

Those walls are reinforced steel. Not even YOU could break through them!

Yeah, you wanna bet?

Step aside, Blackheart.

It's the sidekick we want. Give her up and you needn't be harmed.

A double trap. Clever. I'll give you that one.

However, it seems to me — you're stuck in this trap right along with us.

Ah, but we came prepared.

Bring it on.

144

RAAUUGH

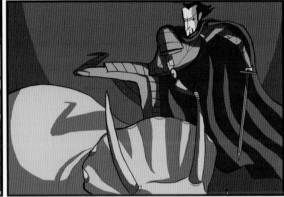

BAM BAM BAM

ZKKT

148

149

150

152

RRRRR

PEW

PEW PEW

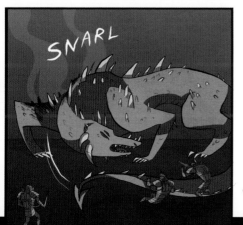

SNARL

RRAUUGHH

SCHWING

NIMONA, GET OUT OF THERE!

154

NIMONA!

ZZZKT

Goldenloin to Director. It's done.

LOCKDOWN COMPLETE. PLEASE STAND BY.

CLANK

CLANK

sorry, Ballister.

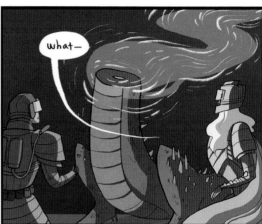

158

BAM

Will you stop...breaking... all my doors...

Let go. I can stand.

Geez, fine. There you go. Knock yourself out.

Whoa!

I didn't mean ACTUALLY knock yourself out.

Augh— my HEAD—

What happened— I don't— How did we—

Don't worry about it.

No—no—they KILLED you. You were DEAD.

Obviously not.

I SAW. I SAW it happen.

Relax. It was a trick. To get them to lift the lockdown.

A trick— but how—

I said don't worry about it.

Goldenloin— is he— did you—

What was I supposed to do? He was trying to kill US.

Nimona, IS HE DEAD?

I don't know.

I'll go find out!

You can't go back out there! It's too dangerous!

NIMONA!

We did everything we could, Director. We didn't have a chance.

She's far more powerful than we thought.

She can't be KILLED.

We assumed she was a girl disguised as a monster, but she's not.

She's a monster disguised as a girl.

I am not interested in excuses. I saw the footage.

You didn't see what I saw.

You didn't see her FACE.

I don't even think Ballister's the one calling the shots anymore. I think she's controlling him somehow.

Whatever the case may be, it is no longer your concern.

You're being replaced.

What are you going to do? You can't FIGHT her.

Fighting her is no longer the plan.

VOIP

END OF CHAPTER NINE

CHAPTER 10

Boss?

Oh, there you are.

Where have YOU been?!

Geez, will you chill out? I TOLD you I was going out to scout around.

What is your problem lately? You've been acting seriously weird all week.

It's looking pretty bleak out there.

You were right, they're definitely censoring the news channels.

They've got the rioters from the tournament locked up— couldn't find out where. Nobody knows.

And here's the kicker—

Two of the people infected with your virus have died.

WHAT?

Whoa!

That's IMPOSSIBLE. I engineered it to be nonlethal!

Well, maybe it's some OTHER mysterious illness then.

But the point is, they're dead.

This has gone on long enough. We have to get the cure to them.

Are you KIDDING?

This is great for us!

Panic is at an all-time high!

Everyone hates the Institution right now!

There won't be a better time to strike. They're disorganized, their star player is in disgrace...

We should attack now and take power from them once and for all.

THEN you can cure the sick people. They'll think you're awesome!

No.

No one else is going to die.

I'm no more fit to rule than the Institution is.

I'm a liar and murderer, and I'm done with this.

166

168

169

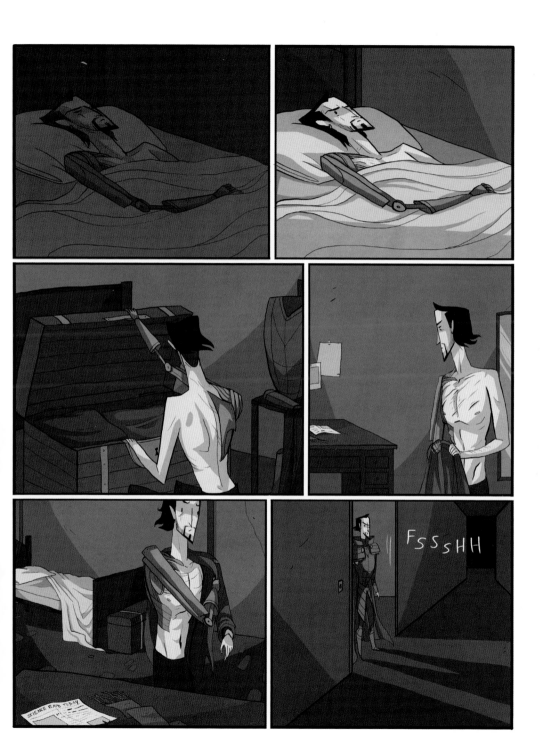

FSSSHH

171

whrrrrr
whrrrr

whrrrrr
whrrrr

CONTACTS

SIR GOLDENLOIN

INSTITUTION - DIREC

NIMONA

CALL FAILED

((🔲))

NIMONA

UNABLE
TO
CONNECT

whrr rr
whrrrr

MEREDITH BLITZMEYER

MAGICAL SCIENTIST*

401 - 0112 - F070

*NOT A WITCH

CALLING

BLITZMEYER LABS

Yes? Hello! Who is it?

Hello, Doctor. We met at the science fair—you gave me your card.

Oh! Gregor, was it? You've cut your beard!

Actually, my name is Ballister Blackheart.

Is it? That's nice.

You don't... recognize me?

I've been on the news a lot lately.

Ah, I don't watch the news! A waste of time.

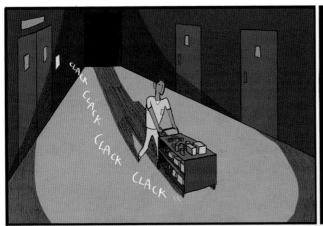

178

179

Where's your sidekick, Ballister?

This again.

She's gone. Are you happy?

Gone where?

I don't know. She LEFT. She's not coming back.

Well, THAT'S a relief.

It looks like you got what you wanted after all.

I'm glad she's gone. You're better off.

She was vicious, she was cruel, she was— EVIL.

So am I.

We both know that's not true.

How'd we end up like this?

You blew up my arm, for one.

...you really do have to bring that up every time, don't you?

Yes.

I just meant... there was a time. Before.

Things were simpler. We were together. It was... good.

It was never that good.

You always remember things as better than they were.

And YOU always remember them as WORSE.

Oh, DO I?

You BETRAYED me. You SHOT me.

I— I never wanted to hurt you. I—

I didn't— It was—

Don't you dare try to tell me again that it was an accident.

It wasn't.

The night before the joust—the Director called me to her office.

She told me that I had promise. That I was her choice for the Institution's Champion.

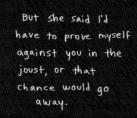

But she said I'd have to prove myself against you in the joust, or that chance would go away.

I wanted it, more than anything. You never wanted it as much as me.

You were just BETTER, without hardly even seeming to try.

Then... on the day of the joust...

This isn't my lance.

Director says it is your lance.

No, it's NOT.

It's weaponized—what does she expect me to do with a weaponized lance?

She expects you to win.

I had no intention of actually USING it...

I was a good rider — you remember.

I knew I could win.

But the new lance was too heavy — it threw me off-balance.

I don't even remember — but I must have —

I'm sorry, Ballister. I'm so sorry.

183

Ballister...

WOOP WOOP WOOP WOOP

RED ALERT. REQUESTING ADDITIONAL PERSONNEL TO SECTION B3. REQUIRED SECURITY CLEARANCE LEVEL SEVEN.

WOOP WOOP WOOP WOOP WOOP WOOP WOOP

what's going on?

Goldenloin to Communications. What's the cause of the alarm? Do you need me to report?

Negative. The situation is under control. Stay where you are.

But what's—

CLK

No one tells me anything.

This armor is atrocious. I hate it.

Do you remember how they used to make us wear that old training armor and they never cleaned it?

This smells like that.

I don't want to talk to you, Ambrosius.

I remember it smelled so bad it made you throw up in the helm.

I didn't do that.

Yes you did!

No, that was— what's his name— Garamond.

Garamond! I forgot about him. He was awful.

Why did you think that was me?

I could've sworn it was you who did that.

I wish— we could just go back. I wish things could be how they were.

We can't. It will never be the same again.

You chose to play along all these years. That doesn't just go away.

Come on. Director's sent for Blackheart.

Where are we?

I don't know. I've never been here before.

Will you stop fraternizing with the enemy?!

Care to show me some respect?

Why should I? I outrank you now.

Clearance code zero-four-nine-six. We have Blackheart.

Will you two pipe down? Now is not the time.

BEEP

Come on, let's go.

WHAM WHAM WHAM WHAM WHAM WHAM WHAM WHAM

What is this place?

What's that noise...?

shut up.

Welcome, Lord Blackheart.

why did you bring me here? what is all this?

I thought you'd be impressed. we've built up quite a collection over the years.

we're on the cutting edge of weapons development.

weapons! For what purpose? The kingdom is not at war.

surely a tactical mind such as your own can appreciate the value of a deterrent.

A dangerous nation is a powerful nation.

188

189

Are you CRAZY, Director, or just stupid?

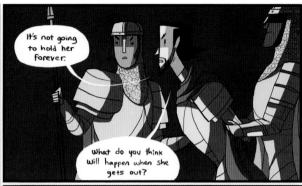

It's not going to hold her forever.

What do you think will happen when she gets out?

She's not going to get out.

ZZKKT

AAAAHHH!

BOSS!

193

194

Have you decided to talk to me?

BLOOD SAMPLE OBTAINED

I want to know who made you, and why.

No?

Shall we give him another shock?

No one made me. I was always like this.

I know an abomination when I see one.

Yeah, sure. What are YOU, a goblin?

That's none of your business.

Shut up.

196

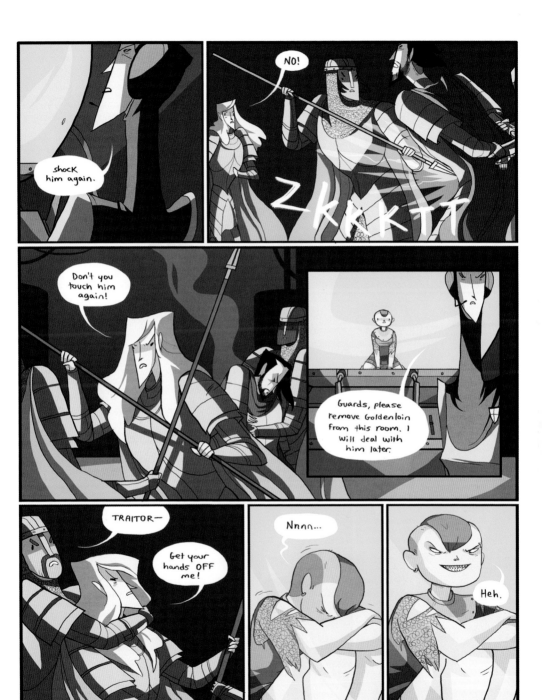

197

198

How's that blood sample looking so far?

Can't see anything special about it myself.

Computer, what's your read on this?

SCANNING SAMPLE.

SCAN RESULT: BLOOD SAMPLE, HUMAN, TYPE AB POSITIVE.

Weird.

There should be some kind of irreg— aaAAAA!

What is it?!

I — it — EXPLODED...

It's—it's growing.

WARNING, EXTREME ACTIVITY DETECTED. OVERLOAD IMMINENT.

— she's still got control over the cells.

AAAHHH!!

Ballister!

RAAAAAUGHH

Nim—

come ON!

FOOOOsHH

205

206

What do you think you're doing?

You can't FIGHT her, Ambrosius, not like that. We've ESTABLISHED this.

What am I supposed to do? She's going to kill a lot of people if we don't stop her.

We have to get back down to the lab—Nimona is still in there!

No, Nimona is OUT THERE, about to destroy the Kingdom!

Part of her is—but part of her never left the cage.

If I can get her out—I can talk to her. Calm her down.

She almost KILLED you, Ballister; she was about to burn you to a crisp.

What makes you think she'll listen to you now?

She's never been exactly STABLE. And now she's really angry.

Oh, and what reason would she have for being ANGRY, I wonder?!

207

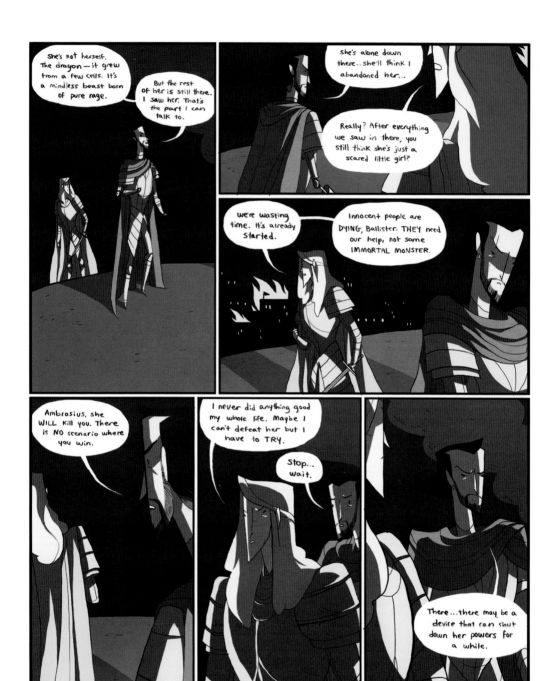

208

209

You can't prioritize her life over theirs.

She's a killer, Ballister. She's always been a killer.

Whether or not you decide to help me, I've got to do SOMETHING.

...No. I can still save her.

I can save them all.

I need to find the device first. Do NOT confront her until I do. She WILL kill you.

You want to be a hero, concentrate on getting the people in the city to safety.

Do you still have that fancy armor?

Somewhere, yes.

You might want to go get it.

CHAPTER 11

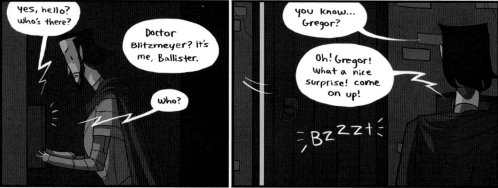

214

Two of our science facilities have been completely destroyed.

It's hit every one of our communication stations, along with the training center and the barracks.

It's looking for you, Director.

BOOOM

I think it found me.

We need to get you out of the city—

I'm NOT running.

I've had about enough of that wretched beast.

Let's see how she likes the taste of jaderoot.

WHHRBR

216

CHOOOM

Come on, then! Have at it!

RAAAUGH

Let's see you grow back from THIS!

FZZKKT

FFFOOON

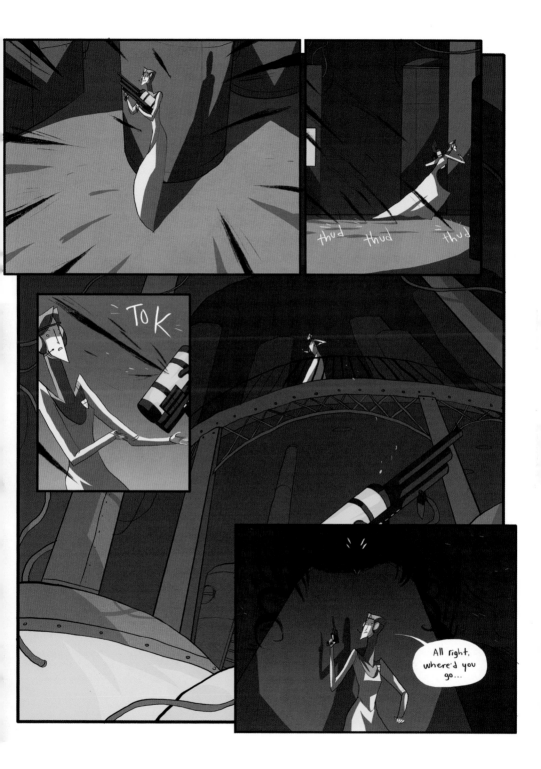

219

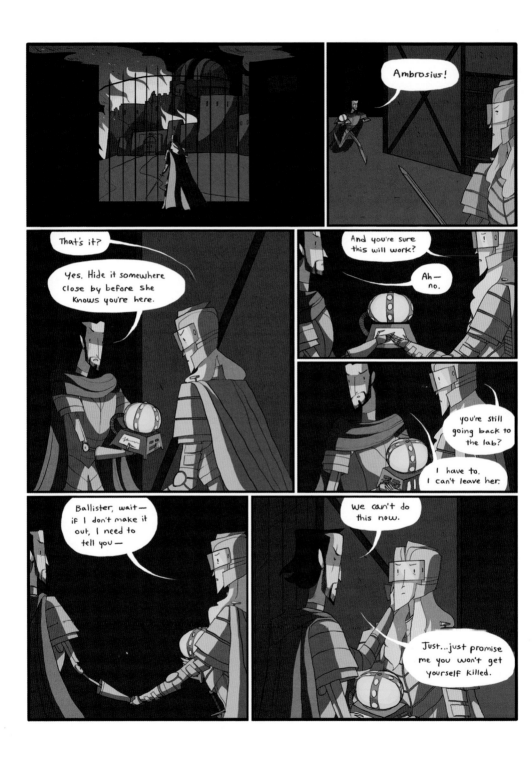

220

221

Half the village saw it happen.

Some even say they saw her breathe fire.

The villagers think she's possessed.

Her parents have a different theory.

They claim that at birth, their daughter was feeble and sick, not expected to live long.

Until, after one particularly dire illness, she quickly recovered and grew into a healthy, robust girl.

Her parents thought nothing of it at the time.

But now they claim this child is an imposter.

That their natural child — the sickly one — is dead, and in its place — something else.

We're going to need a stronger enclosure than this.

Is that really necessary? I mean...

...she's just a kid.

Where's my mom and dad? I want to go home.

Your parents brought you here, didn't they? Why do you think they did that?

I—I burnt a man...

And how did you do that?

I killed them. The raiders.

But they wanted to kill us FIRST. I saved everybody.

I don't know.

You're not going home. Not until you're better. Do you want to get better?

Yes. Then can I see my mom and dad?

Of course.

We'll have her moved to our facility in the morning. Don't upset or excite her in the meantime.

We'll take care of the rest.

228

Y-you're FLAGGING, knight...

You don't look so fresh yourself.

How's it feel to be stuck in one body like the rest of us?

FFFFOOOSSHH

SKID

BOOOOM

233

235

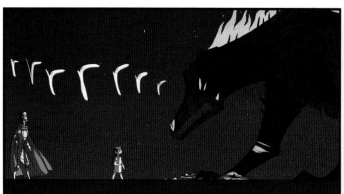

I can't change.

Dammit— the device— I forgot—

They hurt me.

You told them?

hsssss

238

241

242

244

246

He needs a hospital immediately.

Auughh...

Lord Blackheart, what happened? Is the beast slain? Is it over?

Yes.

The Kingdom is in shock after the murderous rampage of a mysterious beast last night that resulted in the deaths of the King and the Director of the Institution.

They are only two out of an extensive list of casualties.

Sir Ambrosius Goldenloin and former villain turned champion of the people Ballister Blackheart brought down the beast early this morning, ending a night of terror.

Both are in the hospital after injuries sustained during the attack. Sir Goldenloin remains in critical condition.

The beast's origins remain unknown, although testimony from surviving employees at Institution headquarters suggests it may be an escaped Institution experiment gone awry.

The catastrophe has brought to light many of the Institution's illegal projects, including the stockpiling of massive quantities of jaderoot.

Prominent voices are already clamoring for the permanent disbanding of the Institution.

Despite this tragedy, we remain united.

We will stay strong, and we will rebuild.

Lord Blackheart? You shouldn't be in here. You need to be resting.

someone should be with him. For when he wakes up.

We don't know if he WILL wake up, m'lord. He's suffered a lot of trauma.

We're monitoring him closely. If his condition changes, we'll know.

Go back to bed. The monster injured you too. You need your rest.

Don't call her that.

m'lord?

She's not a monster.

EPILOGUE

Of course... I still wonder...

...about every stranger who gives me a knowing look.

About every cat who watches me too closely.

I can only hope I reached her in some small way.

I can only hope that if she does come back...

She'll know me for who I am.

A friend.

THANK

YOU!!!

Thanks to my parents and my family for always supporting me and for pushing me to do the things they knew I could do. To Aimee, for always being there to talk me through narrative binds and to give me a shoulder to cry on when I needed one. To Taylor, for always being willing through the years to listen to whatever story I was on fire with at the time. To Charlie and Andrew, for showing incredible faith in a first-time comic creator to bring this book to life. To my sister, for motivating me to tell a better story. To Stephen, for helping me create an online home for Nimona and calmly fielding more than his fair share of panicked emails. To Joan, under whose patient instruction I created the first ten pages and who encouraged me to take the story through to the end. To Esme, Alfred, Sprouts, 2ft1st, redsky, soniadelvalle, Nexus427, Daniel Stubbs, Erin, Joel, FevversAB, Samantha, Rob, Eric, Bear, stickfigurefairytales, Arianod, Spoilersss, Laur, Idris.Ababa, Chris Bishop, ТЯЦТНӨЯD̀ΛЯᴲ, and all the rest of the Tinfoil Brigade, for filling the comments section with lively and good-natured dialogue every week and whose enthusiasm gave me strength. To everyone who supported this comic through the years in such a variety of ways, without whom this story would almost certainly not exist the way it does now. Thank you all, and I love you very much.

The following mini-comics originally appeared in the web comic as Christmas Specials in December 2012 and December 2013.

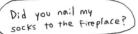

CHRISTMAS

at the
INSTITUTION

BALLISTERRR

What is it?

THOSE BIG DOLTS TOOK MY STOCKING!

Your what?

MY STOCKING. MY CHRISTMAS STOCKING.

How is Father Christmas going to bring me presents without a stocking?!

Okay, calm down. We'll get it back.

I'll call my dad. He'll have them ARRESTED.

You don't have a dad.

Do too. He's rich and lives in a castle far away.

Everyone knows you made that up.

This is why people hit you.

HEY! GIVE HIM BACK HIS STOCKING!

Stocking? You mean my fashionable SOCK?

GASP!

260

261

THE END

DEVELOPMENT OF NIMONA

First ever NIMONA sketches!

NIMONA

1

2

3

woop

Sir Ambrosius Goldenloin   Lord Ballister Blackheart

I'm your new SIDEKICK

NO.

I don't wanna be kept don't wanna be caged don't wanna be damned oh hell

I don't wanna be broke don't wanna be saved don't wanna be S.O.L.

hisssss